IMAGES OF WAR

OPERATION BAGRATION & THE LIBERATION OF MINSK

RARE PHOTOGRAPHS FROM WARTIME ARCHIVES

IMAGES OF WAR

OPERATION BAGRATION & THE LIBERATION OF MINSK

RARE PHOTOGRAPHS FROM WARTIME ARCHIVES

NIK CORNISH

Pen & Sword
MILITARY

First published in Great Britain in 2025 by
PEN & SWORD MILITARY
An imprint of
Pen & Sword Books Ltd
Yorkshire – Philadelphia

ISBN 978 1 03610 578 5

A CIP catalogue record for this book is available from the British Library.

Typeset by Mac Style
Printed in the UK by CPI Group (UK) Ltd, Croydon, CR0 4YY.

MIX
Paper | Supporting responsible forestry
FSC® C013604
www.fsc.org

The Publisher's authorised representative in the EU for product safety is Authorised Rep Compliance Ltd., Ground Floor, 71 Lower Baggot Street, Dublin D02 P593, Ireland.
www.arccompliance.com

For a complete list of Pen & Sword titles please contact

PEN & SWORD BOOKS LIMITED
47 Church Street, Barnsley, South Yorkshire, S70 2AS, England
E-mail: enquiries@pen-and-sword.co.uk
Website: www.pen-and-sword.co.uk
or
PEN AND SWORD BOOKS
1950 Lawrence Road, Havertown, PA 19083, USA
E-mail: uspen-and-sword@casematepublishers.com
Website: www.penandswordbooks.com

'Things fall apart, the centre cannot hold.'

(W. B. Yeats, *The Second Coming*)

This book is dedicated to Liz and to our children James (thanks for the cartography), Charlotte and Alex along with Sebastian, our grandson.

Contents

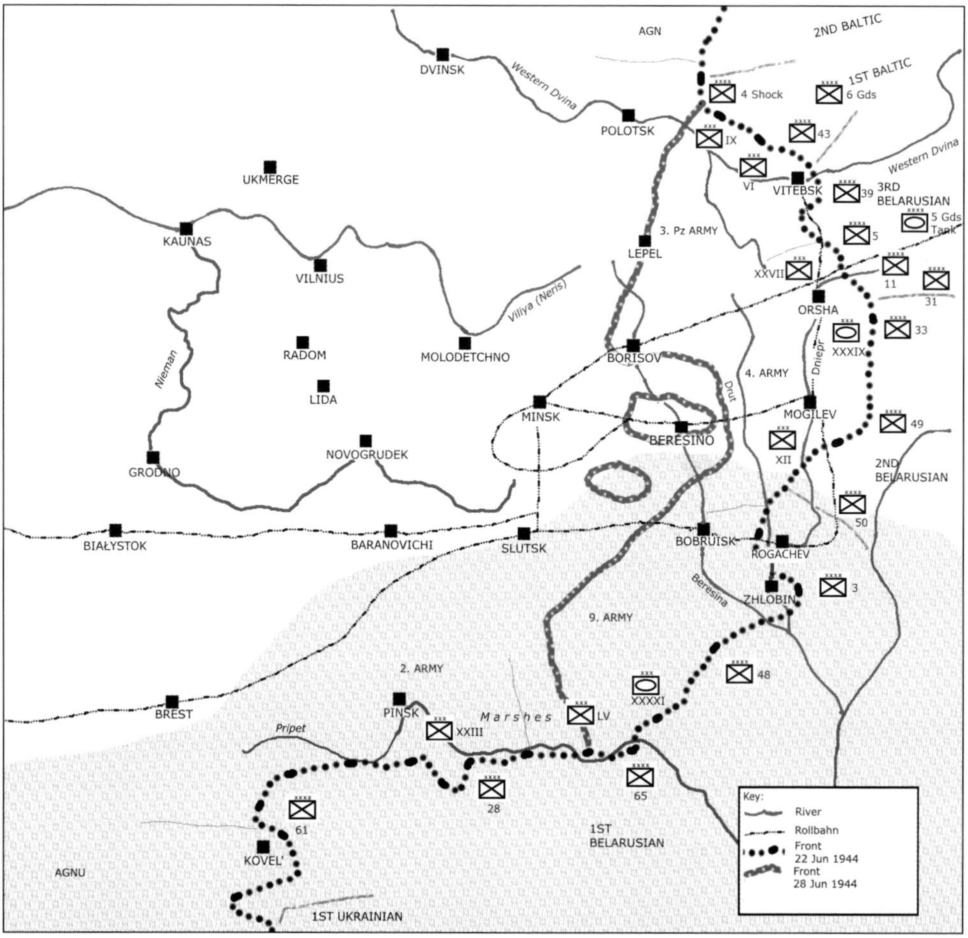

This map shows the position of the frontline on 22 June 1944 and then on 28 June 1944 along with the major rivers, the major *rollbahn* and towns. To avoid overcrowding the maps only German army corps and Red Army armies are shown. Titular armoured formations have an oval inside their box whereas those with a St Andrew's cross are non-armoured formations. The grey shading indicates the Pripet Marshes and other areas of boggy ground.

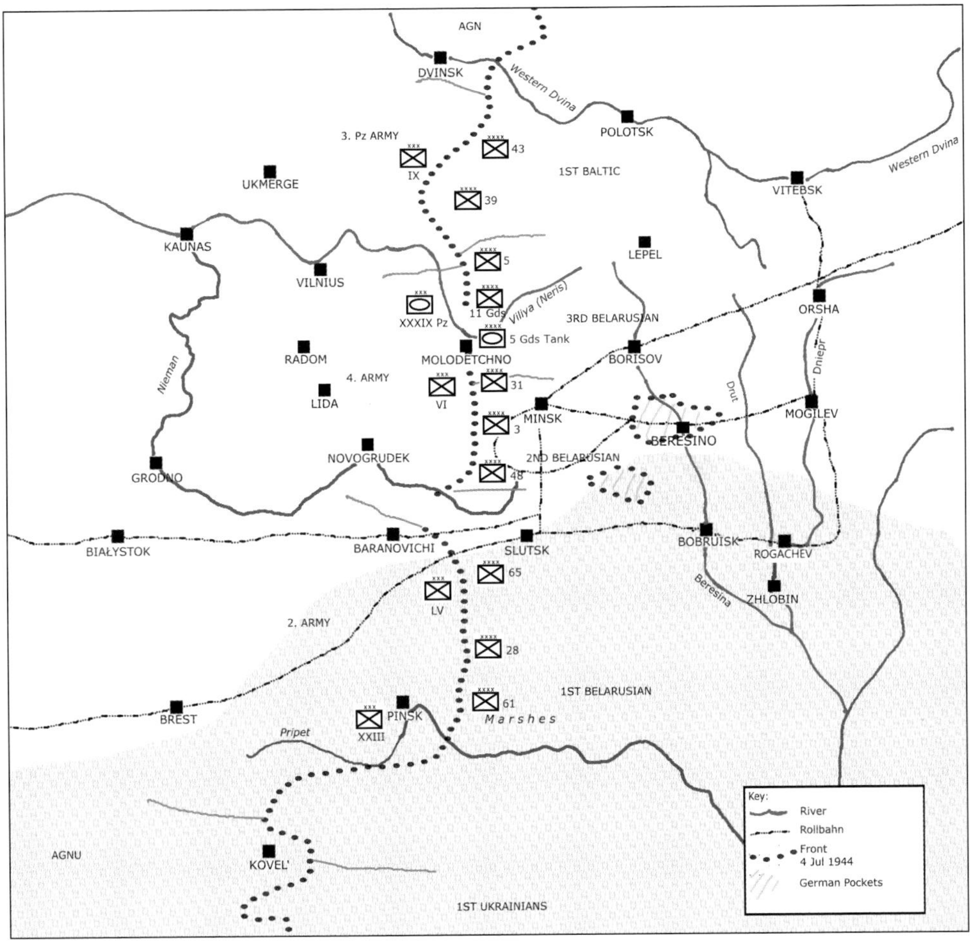

This map shows the position of the frontline on 4 July 1944 along with the major rivers, the major *rollbahn* and towns. Titular armoured formations have an oval inside their box whereas those with a cross are non-armoured formations. The 3rd Baltic Front is not included as it has moved north westwards.

Preface

Operation Bagration is one of the most important offensives undertaken by any Allied army during the Second World War. It was mounted on a scale unprecedented in the history of the Red Army and, during the summer of 1944, broke the back of the Wehrmacht on the Eastern Front. However, it is also one of the great 'unknowns' of military history, certainly in the West. From the opening salvoes that heralded an offensive launched on 9–10 June 1944 that resulted in the eradication of any remaining threat to Leningrad from the Finns to its official end date of 29 August, Bagration achieved colossal gains in terms of territory taken and enemy men and materiel eliminated. So why is it such an unknown in the West? The answer is simple – the Second Front, D-Day, the landings on the beaches of Normandy on 6 June 1944, which took place less than three weeks before the start of the first major phase of Operation Bagration – the assault on Germany's Army Group Centre in Belarus. Nor does it help Westerners that there is so little written about this operation other than it was Hitler's fault because he wouldn't allow a flexible defence. Although this is partially true, it sidesteps the Red Army's involvement somewhat and neatly shifts the blame while almost ignoring the victors. Happily, there is a growing body of work on this topic that is becoming available in the West that gives a broader picture.

The scope of the Red Army's Summer Offensive was immense, stretching from the border with Finland to the Black Sea coast and the border with Romania, a front line of some 1800kms, roughly 1100 miles. When logistical and political requirements brought it to an end, on 29 August 1944, the Red Army had advanced to the suburbs of Warsaw, forced the Finns and Hungarians to step up their search for exit strategies from their arrangements with Germany and decided the Romanians to declare war on Germany. Within less than a year the Third Reich would be in ruins.

Acknowledgements

The usual suspects to whom I am indebted include Dmitry Belanovsky and Norbert Hofer. The debt that I owe to the staff of the Central Museum of the Armed Forces and the Krasnogorsk Archive in Moscow is, as always, immense – thank you all. All images are courtesy of www.Stavka.photos.

Introduction

Given the scale of Operation Bagration, it would be difficult to do it justice in a book of this size. Therefore it is only the opening phase, culminating in the liberation of Minsk, the capital of Belarus (then a part of the USSR), during the first week of July 1944 that we shall be looking at in depth.

Following the defeat of Axis forces at the battle of Stalingrad and the near collapse of Army Group South (AGS) during the winter of 1942–43, the Red Army drove the invaders back towards the Dnepr River, which rises in the Valdai Hills near Smolensk, until the front line was stabilised. However, the bulge in the line that surrounded the city of Kursk provided a tempting target for Germany's limited offensive means.

The Kursk Salient was an obvious target. On a map it stood out like a sore thumb, almost inviting an attack. Therefore, anticipating an attack, and armed with their own and Western intelligence reports, the Soviets spent weeks building deep defensive lines in and around the salient. To this end minefields, natural and man-made anti-tank ditches, anti-tank gun emplacements along all the probable lines of attack and a large armoured reserve to launch against any significant breakthroughs were put in place. The German offensive, Operation Citadel, was launched on 5 July 1943 but proved a costly failure. Having achieved little success, Hitler called off the offensive on 18 July after nearly two of weeks of heavy fighting.

The Soviet counter-blows, a series of offensives to both north and south of the Kursk Salient, were not long in following. Operation Kutuzov struck Army Group Centre (AGC) in mid-July, followed by Operation Rumyantsev at the beginning of August that hit AGS near the city of Belgorod, co-ordinating in a rolling series of staggered attacks that ran down to the Sea of Azov.

Despite anticipating these counter-offensives, the Germans were shocked by their power, strength and ferocity. Consequently, in mid-September, Hitler authorised AGS to fall back to the much-vaunted but virtually non-existent Eastern Rampart defence line that ran along the Dnepr River.

The pressure on AGS was maintained throughout the autumn but, despite desperate counter-attacks, the front line in the south was not stabilised and AGS was forced to assume a defensive posture in early December while striving to maintain its now tenuous links with AGC. Then, on 24 December, to the horror of AGS's command, the Soviets unexpectedly resumed the offensive. Stavka (the Soviet High Command) had resolved to capitalise on its achievements against AGS and scale down its less successful operations against AGC. Furthermore, AGS was looking more and more isolated as its primary, direct rail links with AGC had been cut.

However, the speed of the Soviet winter advance meant that the Red Army was becoming increasingly disorganised and desperately in need of rest and resupply. But Stalin, as was his wont, had demanded more of his men than they were able to deliver. As the spring thaw of 1944 brought the onset of warmer weather, it also ushered in the *rasputitsa* (the 'Muddy Season') that made even the broad-tracked T-34s grind to a halt in the bottomless mud. Consequently, a rejig of plans was undertaken and it was decided to commit Fourth Ukrainian Front (a Front was a group of armies) to the liberation of Crimea, while First, Second and Third Ukrainian Fronts undertook yet another operation against AGS.

All three Ukrainian fronts made good progress, driving AGS back across the Bug River until they were forced to halt along the banks of the Dniester River west of Odessa, which fell on 10 April. No further advance was made in this area due to a stout German defence and the Red Army's need to rest, reorganise and resupply. An operation was also mounted, by Second Belarusian Front, to prevent any attack southwards into the right flank of First Ukrainian Front by AGC.

The front line now ran from Narva, near the Baltic Sea, like a capital letter H with the left up stroke and the right down stroke removed. With Army Group North (AGN) at the top and AGS at the bottom, AGC sat along the centre line of the H and up for about half of the right up stroke resting thus on what the Soviets nicknamed the 'Belarusian Balcony'. The crossbar of the H was drawn across the Pripet Marshes, a vast area of primordial swamp, woodland and forest that was virtually impenetrable by vehicles and home to many Soviet partisan bands.

The failure of AGS to hold the Soviets had not been mirrored by AGC when it faced the Red Army's Operation Kutuzov, which began on 12 July 1943 with the aim of surrounding parts of AGC in the German-held Orel salient, the northern flank of the Kursk Salient. With virtually all of its armoured forces still engaged in the final hours of Operation Citadel, AGC's weak centre seemed ripe for penetration.

However, the terrain east of Orel was not the rolling steppe surrounding Kursk; it was much hillier, heavily wooded and easily defensible. Furthermore, following the invasion of Sicily in mid-July, Hitler's interest in the Eastern Front had been replaced by the fate of Mussolini's Italy. Consequently, he entrusted the defence of Orel to one of his most able officers, *Generaloberst* Walther Model, who now commanded Second Panzer (which had no tanks!) and Ninth Armies. During the course of the next four weeks, Model's forces withdrew steadily and the redeployment of Ninth Army's panzer divisions provided vital reinforcements for counter-attacks. Nevertheless, the liberation of Orel and the reduction of the salient was finally achieved on 5 August and Hitler approved Model's forces' retirement to the Hagen Line. The stage was now set for Stavka's next operation against AGC, the liberation of Smolensk code-named Operation Suvorov. It was anticipated that the fall of Smolensk would present further, unspecified, opportunities. AGC's plan was simply to defend what it held.

AGC's Fourth Army was to bear the brunt of Operation Suvorov. However, it had obtained a useful piece of information that was to prove very valuable. AGC's intelligence section had, due to the poor movement, camouflage and communications security exercised by the opposing Soviet armies, identified the areas under threat seven days before Suvorov began. The Fourth Army's front line was to be the main target, straddling as it did across the relatively well-surfaced Moscow–Minsk highway and several important railway lines some 90km east of Smolensk.

Operation Suvorov's preparatory moves began on 1 August and consisted of a week of partisan attacks on roads and railway lines combined with aerial reconnaissance and bombing raids to gain information and to achieve air superiority.

The partisan operations drew off some forces but the air attacks proved to be a costly failure. When infantry probing attacks began on 6 August, they made little or no headway. This Soviet practice of 'probing with bayonets to find a weak spot' yielded little fresh information on enemy defences but German interrogation of POWs revealed that the start date for Suvorov was 7 August. *Generaloberst* Heinrici, commanding Fourth Army, was thus gifted twenty-four hours to shuffle his meagre reserves to support the positions under threat.

Unfortunately for the Red Army men, the strike force, some thirteen armies drawn from two Fronts, were concentrated into a frontage of roughly 60km. Consequently, there were too many men and too much equipment for the primitive road network to cope with. As one Soviet tank veteran put it, 'some fool in the General Staff planned an operation where … the terrain there was forested swamp'. In addition, Soviet artillery fire plans were, by this time, quite predictable, resulting in wasted ammunition for few enemy losses due to the front-line troops withdrawing out of range. Therefore, despite their considerable superiority in men and materiel, it took the Red Army six weeks to liberate Smolensk, which it accomplished on 25 September. Stavka had hoped to advance further in the direction of Orsha, Vitebsk and Mogilev but little was achieved. The last town of any consequence to be taken was Nevel, which fell on 6 October.

At this point the Soviet fronts were ordered to halt operations. Despite having driven AGC back, in some places over 200km, it was not a broken force and in Moscow Stalin was not a happy man. The Stavka representative and Co-ordinator of the Fronts involved, Chief Marshal of Artillery N. N. Voronov, was removed, as were several other senior officers. The next time AGC was to face a major Soviet offensive, so Stavka determined, it would be undertaken differently.

On the German side of the line, command of AGC was placed in the hands of *Generalfeldmarschall* Ernst Busch and there were to be other command changes over the following months. However, AGC now had time to fortify its positions and attempt to rebuild its depleted units. The Red Army was also granted time to learn from the miscalculations and blunders of the recent fighting in the centre and to prepare for the campaigns of 1944.

The crushing defeat suffered by Army Groups South and Centre at the battle of Kursk in July 1943 massively reduced Germany's capacity to wage more than reactive, defensive operations. Here a group of senior Red Army officers inspects an abandoned SdKfz 184 tank destroyer, better known as an Elefant, on the northern flank of the Kursk Bulge. Such defensive weaponry symbolised Germany's move towards a more defensive stance on the Eastern Front. General of the Army K. K. Rokossovsky can be seen at the front of the central group. (*Courtesy of the Central Museum of the Armed Forces, Moscow via Stavka*)

Throughout the autumn and winter of 1943 and into the spring of 1944 the Wehrmacht was in almost continuous retreat. The Germans and their allies carried out a comprehensive scorched earth policy. Nothing was to be left standing that would aid the advancing Red Army. Here German troops leave a blazing village. (*Nik Cornish at www.stavka.photos*)

The ground defended by AGC was wooded, hilly and lacked good roads. Here a 76mm Soviet light regimental gun M1928 is manoeuvred into position. Production was halted in late 1943 but it remained in service as a close-support weapon with infantry units. Although heavy, it was robust and reliable. (*Nik Cornish at www.stavka.photos*)

A 380mm gun of the Todt Battery at Cap Griz-Nes formed part of the Atlantic Wall in France in 1944. On 3 November 1943 Hitler had ordered (Fuhrer Directive 51) that the defensive build-up in the west should take priority over the needs of the Eastern Front. Kiev was liberated three days later. As well as static defences, the number of armoured units in the west was to be increased considerably. (*Nik Cornish at www.stavka.photos*)

Soviet gunners manning a 122mm gun M1931/37 are briefed on the latest news by the unit's Political Officer (Politruk). With more than twelve months of success behind them, the morale of the Red Army was at an all-time high and it was the job of Political Officers to maintain this as well as encouraging Party membership and political correctness. (*From the fonds of the RGAKFD in Krasnogorsk via Stavka*)

By the summer of 1944 the VVS (the Russian acronym for Military Air Force) enjoyed air superiority due to the priority given to defending the Reich, which drained vital resources. Here two Yak-1 fighters carry out a routine patrol. Ironically, AGC's Luftflotte 6 had a unit of former VVS pilots on its strength until disbanded in early July. Sadly, there is little known of this formation other than it flew over 500 combat missions during its twelve-month existence. (*Courtesy of the Central Museum of the Armed Forces, Moscow via Stavka*)

Chapter One

Plans and Preparations

Soviet Planning

By early 1944 it was clear that the strategic initiative lay firmly in the hands of the Red Army. As Stalin put it in his speech on May Day 1944: 'As a result of the successful offensive, the Red Army has emerged on our State frontiers on a stretch of more than 400km and liberated more than three quarters of occupied Soviet land from the German fascist yoke. The aim now is to clear the whole of our land from the fascist invaders and to re-establish the State frontiers of the Soviet Union along the entire line from the Black Sea to the Barents Sea.'

What he did not mention was that the first formal discussions regarding the upcoming summer operations had begun on 5 April.

Three options had been discussed. First, an invasion of the Balkans via Romania, second a thrust towards the Baltic Sea from north-western Ukraine and third a head-on strike into Belarus with AGC and Minsk, the capital of Belarus, as the main targets. After due consideration, options one and two were ruled out, mainly because they would expose one or both flanks to counter-attacks and would not lead to the liberation of the last major region of the USSR still in Axis hands – Belarus. Furthermore, success in Belarus would open up possibilities for operations towards both the Baltic States and the Balkans with secure flanks. This option also presented the chance of isolating AGN and penetrating the German province of East Prussia, which would provide the morale-boosting propaganda coup of Red Army boots on the territory of the Third Reich for the first time as well as opening the most direct, practicable route to Berlin itself.

On 12 April Stalin and the State Defence Council (the wartime ruling body of the USSR) approved the third option. The order was then issued to all Fronts to cease aggressive operations. Stavka, the armed forces High Command, headed by Stalin, with Marshal of the Soviet Union G. K. Zhukov as his deputy, was ordered to begin planning for the summer offensives. Bagration (a Georgian who fought for Russia during the Napoleonic Wars) was to be the code name for the Belarusian operation. It was one of a series of rolling, staggered offensives that would begin in early June. The first operation would be launched against Finland.

However, Bagration, with the liberation of Minsk as its initial objective, was to be the first of the major operations and was scheduled to begin on 19 June.

In his memoirs, General of the Army K. K. Rokossovsky, commanding First Belarusian Front, describes the offensive plans as follows: 'The forces of four fronts were given important strategic and political objectives: to liquidate the enemy's salient in the Vitebsk, Bobruisk, Minsk area, defeat and rout AGC, liberate the Belarusian Soviet Republic … Great importance was attached to effective coordination, especially between the Third and First Belarusian fronts, whose troops were to advance rapidly westward in a pincer movement that was to close west of Minsk.'

What Rokossovsky was describing sounds simple and in effect it was. The first attacks would break through the German defences, forcing them to retreat. By maintaining this pressure, the Germans would be unable to reform a cohesive defence line and, when the enemy's position was judged to be sufficiently disordered, the Soviet commanders would unleash their Cavalry-Mechanised formations to exploit the situation and penetrate the German rear, sowing further chaos. By maintaining the speed of the advance, keeping the Germans off balance and unable to stabilise defence lines, and denying them the opportunity to counter-attack, so did Stavka intend to achieve its aims. This form of attack was in line with Soviet military doctrine dating back to the mid-1920s and was known as the Deep Operations Theory. Elements of it had been implemented during the conflict with Japan in the 1930s. However, as many of the proponents of Deep Operations had been purged in the late 1930s, it had fallen out of favour as politically unacceptable. The consequence was that different ideas dominated the first year or so of fighting on the Eastern Front until Deep Operations were resurrected and used in action during the winter of 1942–43. Although these methods were successful, the Red Army needed to hone its application, which it did during the course of the next twelve months, learning by often bitter and bloody experience. Operation Bagration would witness the extent to which Stavka and the Front commanders along with their subordinates had taken these lessons to heart and were to exploit them.

When a multi-Front operation was to be undertaken, it was Stavka's practice to assign one or more co-ordinators to oversee the operation. Stavka had appointed Chief Marshal of Artillery N. N. Voronov as its representative during Operation Suvorov. His criticism of the manner in which this was undertaken was highly relevant as much of Bagration would be carried out over similar terrain and with many of the same formations and challenges as Suvorov. Voronov wrote: 'OKH [Germany's High Command of the Army] knew all about the operation and was prepared for it. German defence lines were exceptionally well prepared … Several Red Army rifle divisions [all Soviet infantry units were referred to as Rifle] were insufficiently prepared to perform an assault on a multi-layered defence zone … training was not always properly supervised. There were not enough tanks committed to battle … the interaction between regiments and division was far from perfect … and [there was] a strong will of some regiments to 'hide' from the attack and expose another regiment. Many Red Army commanders were too impressed by Wehrmacht counter-attacks and failed to act properly. The infantry were not using their own weapons [such as their own heavy guns and portable mortars] well enough.' Stavka took Voronov's advice to heart.

From the outset, planning was carried out in total secrecy, the details being held by fewer than a dozen individuals. To protect information about planning and preparation at all levels, from the lowliest Ivan in the front line to the most senior of staff officer in the Kremlin, a tightly enforced Maskirovka (deception and camouflage) operation was launched.

To ensure security at all levels, radio traffic was cut to a minimum, important information was passed by telephone or courier and then only between specified personnel on a strictly need to know basis. Troop movements were carried out at night, particularly the movement of vehicle-heavy units such as Fifth Guards Tank Army from southern Ukraine. Vehicles, particularly tanks, would only travel at night and personnel were issued with special passes that did not include their unit designations. Indeed, when AGC's Ninth Army reported a build-up of Soviet forces near the front, it was dismissed as a deception.

The Red Army's main attacks would be preceded by a wave of sabotage, intelligence gathering and generally distracting partisan missions aimed at multiple points across the rear of AGC. This would begin on 19 June. The partisans would continue to fight alongside the Red Army proper when its operations began.

Four Fronts, which were, from north to south, First Baltic Front, Third, Second Belarusian Fronts and significant elements of First Belarusian Front's right wing, were to be involved in Bagration. First Baltic Front (commander General of the Army I. Kh. Bagramyan) included the Fourth Shock, Sixth Guards, Forty-Third and Third Air Armies; the Third Belarusian Front (Colonel General I. D. Chernyakhovsky) comprised the Eleventh Guards Army, Fifth, Thirty-First, Thirty-Ninth, Fifth Guards Tank and First Air Armies; the Second Belarusian Front (Colonel General G. F. Zakharov) included the Thirty-Third, Forty-Ninth, Fiftieth and Fourth Air Armies. The First Belarusian Front (General of the Army K. K. Rokossovsky) contributed the Third, Twenty-Eighth, Forty-Eighth, Sixty-First, Sixty-Fifth, Sixth Air and Sixteenth Air Armies. Stavka chose Marshals of the Soviet Union G. K. Zhukov and A. M. Vasilevsky to co-ordinate the First and Second Belarusian Fronts and Third Belarusian and First Baltic Fronts respectively.

Numerically, the Soviets fielded almost 1,700,000 ground troops, roughly 4,000 armoured vehicles and more than 5,000 combat aircraft.

The initial tactical objectives were Vitebsk, Mogilev, Orsha and Bobruisk. The liberation of Minsk and the destruction of the German forces looming over the Red Army in the Belarusian Balcony were the main objectives of the first phase of Bagration.

The four Fronts would not launch their attacks simultaneously but would follow in sequence so as to confuse the movement of German reserves. The first attack would be launched towards Vitebsk by First Baltic Front on 19 June, followed by the Third and Second Belarusian Fronts later that day and then, on 20 June, First Belarusian Front's right wing as it would not be committing to operations against the entirety of Second Army's positions. The length of the line along which the Soviet Fronts would be launching their main attacks was roughly 700km. The left wing of First Belarusian Front was to be held in waiting as it would be committed directly westwards towards Lublin to break the connection between AGNU and AGC when the time was right. In brief, the general plan was to crush the flanks of the AGC, encircle its main forces east of Minsk and destroy them and then completely liberate Belarus.

When the first phase of Bagration was completed, the fronts to the north and south, Second Baltic Front and the left wing of First Belarusian Front, would be unleashed to drive AGN out of the Baltic States and AGNU back into Poland. Although there was a timetable for Bagration's first phase, it would be subject to constant review as the operational situation developed.

However, due to logistical problems, the first phase of Bagration was postponed until 22 June. This did not impact the start of the partisans' activities, which began on schedule.

German Planning

As the Red Army went into defensive mode with the onset of the *rasputitsa* so, on 5 April 1944, AGS was split into two with the creation of Army Group North Ukraine (AGNU) and Army Group South Ukraine. (AGSU). The left flank of AGNU connected with AGC's right flank close by Kovel. AGNU was commanded by, now *Generalfeldmarschall*, Walter Model, AGSU by *Generaloberst* Ferdinand Schörner.

From October 1943 AGC had been commanded by *Generalfeldmarschall* Ernst Busch. Busch, an ardent and committed Nazi, was very much in Hitler's thrall, prepared to obey his orders to the letter and almost without question.

In early May, *Fremde Heere Ost* (FHO), the intelligence branch of OKH, had predicted two likely directions for the Soviet summer offensive: one into the Balkans, the other into the Kovel area towards Warsaw and the Baltic coast.

Of these, the Balkan direction was considered the most advantageous for the Red Army as it would realise the Soviet Union's long hoped for control of south-eastern Europe. Nevertheless, the prospect of a secondary Soviet offensive between the Carpathian Mountains and the Pripet Marshes, near Kovel, remained a distinct possibility due to a marked increase in the amount of railway traffic in the area. Consequently, FHO's final assessment of the situation regarding AGC and the Belarusian Balcony was that it would remain quiescent. Furthermore, any attacks that were directed against it would be diversionary and that AGNU was the target at which the Red Army would aim its summer offensive.

Unbeknownst to OKH, these options had both been rejected by the State Defence Council on 12 April. Indeed, the railway movements facing Kovel were part of the Red Army's *maskirovka*. Further proof of the *maskirovka*'s success came in late May when AGNU's intelligence officers again reported that it was to be the target of the Soviet summer offensive when they confirmed further significant increases in rail traffic. AGC was definitely not, in FHO or OKH's opinion, to be subjected to anything more than minor attacks.

One of the most significant consequences of FHO's assessment was that AGNU's commander Model requested the transfer of AGC's major armoured formation LVI Panzer Corps to AGNU. The Führer agreed to this on 20 May. As it was an order from Hitler, Busch did not protest and at a stroke AGC lost 88 per cent of its tanks, 23 per cent of its assault guns, 50 per cent of its tank destroyers and one third of its heavy artillery.

On 24 May Busch summoned his army commanders to a conference to impress on them that the Führer's order that the Panther Line, along AGC's eastern front following the Dnepr River, was to be held at all costs and that defence building should now focus on the front line at the expense of support lines further back. Despite the intelligence now coming in from all of the armies under his command, from the junction with AGN Third

Panzer (*Generaloberst* Georg-Hans Reinhardt) Fourth (General Kurt von Tippelskirch), Ninth (General Hans Jordan) and Second (*Generaloberst* Walter Weiß) that connected with AGNU armies, that the Soviet formations to their fronts were receiving large numbers of new units, Busch remained unmoved. Indeed it has been suggested that he refused to pass these reports on to either OKH or FHO. Both OKH's and FHO's attention were now focussed on AGNU and how it would deal with the anticipated Soviet attack. Busch's and thus AGC's planning consisted of no more than following Hitler's instructions to hold the front precisely where it stood. The best description of the situation in which it found itself is the following quotation from Ninth Army's war diary entry of 22 June 1944: '... in the last few weeks the enemy has completed an assembly on the very grandest scale opposite the army, and the army is convinced that that overshadows the concentration of forces off the northern flank of AGNU ... The army believes that, even under the present conditions, it would be possible to stop the enemy offensive, but not under the present directives which require an absolute rigid defence ... if a Soviet offensive breaks out the army will either have to go over to a mobile defence or see its front smashed ... The army considers the orders establishing the Fortified Places [*Feste Platz*] particularly dangerous.'

Feste Platz were Hitler's idea, as outlined in Führer Order 11 of 8 March 1944. The idea was simple: create fortresses that were not to be given up at any cost during an enemy offensive. As Hitler put it, 'They have to allow themselves to be surrounded and thereby tie down the strongest possible enemy forces. In doing so, you have to help create the conditions for successful counter-operations.' Hitler's optimism was based on his belief that the long-anticipated invasion of France would be defeated by a powerful armoured strike and the Eastern Front would hold firm. With the Western Allies driven back into the sea, the victorious panzers would then be transferred to the Eastern Front, where, it was hoped, they would repeat their success against the Red Army. The Führer's thinking had overtones of the Schlieffen Plan, when the defeat of France in six weeks would release the majority of Germany's forces to crush Russia. But this was not 1914, nor did Busch enjoy the operational freedom that his predecessors had exploited in East Prussia, resulting in the German victory at Tannenberg.

Feste Platz were to be chosen for their operational importance as transport hubs, their potential use as bridgeheads or other particular strategic, political or prestige value. Führer Order 11 included the names of twenty-nine *Feste Platz*, of which eight were in AGC's area. These were, from the connection point with AGN to the link point with AGNU, Vitebsk, Orsha, Mogilev, Bobruisk, Slutsk and Pinsk: roughly 120km west from Orsha, along the rail and surfaced road (the latter was termed Rollbahn in German military parlance) link to *Feste Platz* Minsk, lay Borisov. Borisov, 70km east of Minsk, was designated a *Feste Platz* as it was the major crossing point for both the road and rail links with the west over the upper reaches of the Berezina River. Vitebsk was a bridgehead across the Western Dvina River, Orsha and Mogilev bridgeheads on the Dnepr River and Bobruisk across the lower Berezina River. Worryingly, there was no significant bridging point across the Berezina between Bobruisk and Borisov, roughly 110km of frequently marshy ground. If German forces were driven back in that direction then time would be required to erect bridges.

Although there had been no major Soviet operations against AGC's positions along the Dnepr River, there had been several attacks following the end of Operation Suvorov, generally directed at Fourth Army, the intention being to breakthrough either at Orsha or Mogilev and dash for Minsk. None of these attempts made any ground due to the skilful defensive tactics and the ability of the defenders to move reserves from Third Panzer Army to the north and Ninth Army to the south, neither of which was under direct threat.

However, denuded of its main armoured strength in late May, lacking aircraft due to transfers to home defence and Western Europe and short of infantry, AGC was not the force it had been during the early months of the year when it had contained the Soviet attacks. Indeed, it is arguable that AGC was a victim of its own recent successes. Nevertheless, with AGNU the apparent target of Stalin's summer operations, AGC was to be subjected to mere diversionary attacks that, so it was anticipated, it would hold with relative ease, with defending the 1,100km line as it was to be the full extent of AGC's planning.

AGC's order of battle included thirty-four infantry, two Panzer Grenadier, and two Luftwaffe field divisions (LFD), 20th Panzer Division, the understrength Panzer Grenadier Division *Feldhernnhalle* and a hotchpotch collection of rear area security, police and training units. The removal of LVI Panzer Corps had reduced its armoured force to ninety tanks and 579 StuG III assault guns. These figures include those under repair. Not included in these figures were specialist tank destroyers (*Panzerjäger*) vehicles such as the Marder and Hornisse. On 22 June 1944 AGC's reserve consisted of the 14th and *Feldhernnhalle* Panzer Grenadier divisions, 20th Panzer Division and 707th Security Division. This resource gave Busch very little flexibility to support his *Feste Platz* and launch the expected counter-attacks. If the Red Army did not follow OKH's plan for it then AGC faced a daunting summer to say the least.

Red Army infantry advance cautiously towards a Finnish position. This first phase of the Soviet summer offensive was a relatively small undertaking designed to push the Finns out of the war, drive into Karelia and remove any threat to Leningrad. It began on 10 June, proved highly successful and during early August both Soviet Fronts involved assumed defensive postures. On 19 September the USSR and Finland concluded an armistice. (*Courtesy of the Central Museum of the Armed Forces, Moscow via Stavka*)

Creating a series of *Feste Platz* with the stroke of a pen does nothing for the men tasked with making this a reality. In theory each *Feste Platz* would have a skeleton garrison that would increase to two divisions (three for Vitebsk). This would immobilise 50 per cent of AGC's divisions. Furthermore, the swampy nature of the terrain and rain did not help the building of such positions. However, semi-continual partisan activity reduced the number of men available for work, training or rest. (*Nik Cornish at www.stavka.photos*)

As well as a lack of armoured units, AGC was also weak in infantry. Many of its formations were chronically understrength and, of those, a high proportion were security troops who were poorly equipped as well as training and rear-echelon formations, all of which were generally unsuited for front-line duties. There were also two divisions formed from surplus Luftwaffe ground crew such as the men seen here. (*Nik Cornish at www.stavka.photos*)

The T-34, offloading a group of infantrymen, is carrying tree trunks to facilitate crossing streams and boggy areas. Recovery tanks, old T-34s with the turret removed, were ordered to carry logs, as seen here, and a 4m section of bridge. As there were five recovery vehicles to each tank brigade, the resulting 20m bridge was a vital asset to speed up the advance. (*From the fonds of the RGAKFD in Krasnogorsk via Stavka*)

The profusion of waterways and marshes that criss-crossed Belarus led to intensive training in the crossing of such obstacles. Rokossovsky noted, 'Men learned to swim, cross swamps and rivers with any available means … Helped by engineers the (tank) crews provided each tank with faggots, logs and special triangles [fascines] for crossing ditches.' Vehicle crossings were also built beneath the surface of waterways so that they could not be spotted from the air. (*Nik Cornish at www.stavka.photos*)

The German front line, trenches and trees. AGC anticipated holding Soviet attacks along the courses of the Dnepr and then the Berezina rivers, which were the main rivers running through the area roughly parallel with one another until the Berezina flowed into the Dnepr just within the Soviet lines about 50km south of Zhlobin. (*Nik Cornish at www.stavka.photos*)

Up to one third of Belarus consisted of semi-primeval marsh and forest. The major area of wetland, the Pripet Marshes, is roughly 260,000 square kilometres in area. This morass separated First Belarusian Front from AGC's Second Army and the right flank of Ninth Army. Home to thousands of refugees and partisans, it was navigable by sunken paths and occasional dirt roads connecting the few settlements. (*Nik Cornish at www.stavka.photos*)

Many of the main roads were not much better than tracks. Here a Panzer II escorts a supply column along a typical road to protect it against the partisans. A senior German staff officer described the main paved road, the Moscow–Minsk highway, as unable to support trucks that often, 'broke through the (tarmac) pavement up to their axles'. (*Nik Cornish at www.stavka.photos*)

III Guards Tank Corps deployed Sherman M4 tanks provided under the Lend-Lease scheme. The Sherman was popular with Soviet crews as they were less prone to rounds 'cooking off' if hit, plus they were more comfortable to ride in. It was also noticeably quieter than Soviet armour. *(Courtesy of the Central Museum of the Armed Forces, Moscow via Stavka)*

AGC's armoured component included Heavy Panzer Battalion 501. These specialist units consisted of roughly forty-five Tiger I tanks. The 501st was ordered to transfer nine Tigers to AGNU, thus reducing it to twenty operational vehicles by 22 June. (*Nik Cornish at www.stavka.photos*)

A T34/76 model 1943 with its neatly posed crew. This tank formed the backbone of the Soviet tank fleet during Bagration. Uncomfortable within and physically demanding to operate efficiently in combat, it was nevertheless one of the best tanks of its day. The turret logo reads, 'Trade Union of Consumer Cooperation Centre'. Many civilian bodies clubbed together to buy a tank such as this one. (*Courtesy of the Central Museum of the Armed Forces, Moscow via Stavka*)

By far the mainstay of AGC's armoured forces was the StuG III, of which there were 579 available in June 1944. The vehicles shown here have the wider tracks for soft ground crossing and added armour plate skirts (*Schürzen*) to protect the running gear. In ambush situations its powerful 75mm anti-tank gun proved its worth time and again. (*Nik Cornish at www.stavka.photos*)

In November 1943 Hitler ordered the creation of the *Nationalsozialistischer Führungsoffizier* (NSFO; National Socialist Leadership Officers). These were to be selected officers, sometimes NCOs, who would be made responsible for political education with a view to improving the morale and motivation of their men. Here one such holds forth on the Nazi mission to a group of men. (*Nik Cornish at www.stavka.photos*)

No matter how much effort the upper echelons of the Red Army put into *Maskirovka*, the ordinary Ivans were well aware of what increased political education and the issue of new underclothes presaged – a major attack. This unit's politruk is speaking to an audience that looks remarkably disinterested despite the presence of the camera. (*From the fonds of the RGAKFD in Krasnogorsk via Stavka*)

Far behind the lines an Il-2 Shturmovik warms up under light camouflage netting. Closer to the front the camouflage would have been much denser. Roughly 1,700 Shturmovik ground-attack aircraft were deployed for Operation Bagration. For security reasons up to half of these aircraft were not flown to forward airbases until twenty-four hours before Bagration started. One of their major roles was neutralising German artillery positions. (*Courtesy of the Central Museum of the Armed Forces, Moscow via Stavka*)

The majority of German artillery was horse drawn and this handicapped its ability to execute fire/move tactics. The lack of transport also hampered the resupply of ammunition. This gun crew is ranging in on a traffic choke point, with such targets being prioritised. (*Nik Cornish at www.stavka.photos*)

Chapter Two

Target Vitebsk

Operation Bagration was to be preceded by a wave of attacks by partisan units that were intended to disrupt German lines of communications, gather information and sow confusion behind the front lines. Furthermore, the partisans were expected to provide guidance through the swamps and forests for Red Army forces, harass and delay German reinforcements or retreating units, mine roads and generally support the regular troops in any way possible when the offensive was under way.

Belarus was home to the largest number of partisans, certainly in Axis-occupied regions of the USSR if not in occupied Europe. There were two main reasons for this: the large number of uncaptured troops cut off by the speed of the German advance in 1941 and the vast areas of forests and swamps that gave refuge to those, both soldier and civilian, who wished to fight on against the invaders.

By the spring of 1944 the Belarusian partisan formations were a relatively well-equipped and highly organised movement, frequent German anti-partisan sweeps notwithstanding. The number of units and their membership is debatable but there were certainly tens of thousands of fighters grouped into brigades that were sub-divided into detachments. Indeed, there were large areas of Belarus that were effectively controlled by the partisans despite the punitive operations launched by German security units and their collaborationist auxiliaries. Indeed, there were many instances of Belarusian police units fighting Belarusian partisans.

The partisan offensive was scheduled to begin on 19 June, at the same time as the Red Army started Bagration itself. However, the postponement of the Red Army's attack did not alter the partisan operation, which went ahead as planned. Road and rail movements were disrupted, rear area bases were attacked and intelligence gathering was undertaken. It is difficult to compare post-war Soviet claims for the effectiveness of the partisans with the reality but there is no doubt that they had an effect at a time when AGC's resources were stretched. Nor did such missions come to an end when Bagration proper began. If anything, the partisans increased their efforts as, within a few short days, it was becoming clear that the Red Army was unlikely to fail in achieving its objectives and no one wished to be accused of a lack of courage or commitment to the cause of Soviet victory or that most heinous of crimes – collaboration.

The first Soviet objective was the destruction of Third Panzer Army, severing AGC's connection with AGN and the liberation of Vitebsk and Orsha. First Baltic Front and elements of Third Belarusian Front were committed to these operations. Nor was the protection of the flank from AGN ignored.

During the night of 22–23 June, First Baltic Front's Sixth Guards and Forty-Third Armies launched a series of company- and battalion-sized reconnaissance and probing attacks searching for weak points in the German line from Vitebsk to a point roughly 70km north where AGC and AGN connected just north-east of Polotsk. Operation Bagration's first phase had begun and Vitebsk, in *Generaloberst* Reinhardt's Third Panzer Army's zone, was its main target as it was the core of a bridgehead across the Western Dvina River and the point at which several road, rail and water routes coincided. The city was also one of Hitler's *Feste Platz,* therefore it was to be held to the last man. Although a Panzer Army, Reinhardt's force did not possess one tank. Its armour consisted of three assault gun brigades numbering just seventy-six StuG IIIs.

Vitebsk was, as a Soviet writer noted, 'a protrusion on a protrusion', jutting out as it did from the tip of the Belarusian Balcony to create the Western Dvina Bridgehead.

A weak spot was identified in General Wuthmann's IX Army Corps' (AC) sector near the village of Sirotino, north-west of Vitebsk, and there a breach was made that rapidly grew to some 8km wide by 5km deep. Wuthmann requested permission to withdraw. Busch refused, stating, 'nothing was to be abandoned that could be lost in battle'. Hitler's recipe for disaster was about to be tasted. By evening the salient had grown and IX AC found itself under increasing pressure, as did Third Panzer Army south of Vitebsk where Third Belarusian Front had joined the fray, striking at Third Panzer Army's VI AC, preceded by the usual reconnaissance in force. Third Belarusian Front's main attack started late on 22 June, earlier than planned, to exploit the achievements further north. Units of Fifth and Sixth Guards Armies had penetrated German defences, the latter to a depth of 7km.

Elsewhere, things had not gone so well for Chernyakhovsky's forces. But now German Fourth Army was involved as men of Chernyakhovsky's Eleventh Guards Army struck at 78th 'Sturm' (Assault) Division, one of AGC's strongest formations, defending the Moscow–Minsk highway. Another of AGC's stronger formations, 25th Panzer Grenadier Division, with forty or so StuG IIIs, held its right flank. As well as covering the Minsk highway, which ran through terrain more suited for armoured warfare, these divisions were involved in defending *Feste Platz* Orsha and the bridgehead over the Dnepr River.

Eleventh Guards Army was ordered to break through enemy defences to open the Minsk highway, which in turn would open the route to Minsk for the Fifth Guards Tank Army led by Marshal of the Armoured Forces P.A. Rotmistrov. However, as the attacks were not progressing well it was decided to move Rotmistrov's armour to a different jumping off point to launch its attack when Fifth Army's efforts created an opportunity.

Fourth Army's commander, General Kurt von Tippelskirch, had already made several requests to withdraw his forces to the defensive positions west of the Dnepr River but all had been refused by Busch. However, Busch did send a regiment from Panzer Grenadier Division *Feldhernnhalle* to take up support positions on the west bank of the Dnepr, while at the same time moving 14th Infantry Division from Fourth Army's reserve to Third

Panzer Army, robbing Peter to pay Paul! Tippelskirch was also reminded that his forces were expected to stand firm; flexible defensive tactics were ruled out.

The transfer of 14th Infantry Division was, unfortunately for Third Panzer Army, too little too late as by the morning of 24 June it was clear that the gap between VI AC and LIII AC, the southern and central units respectively, was irreparable despite numerous counter-attacks. IX AC, which connected AGC with AGN, was ordered to hold the line of the Western Dvina River but Soviet pressure was such that it was lucky to reach the river without being encircled and, despite receiving reinforcements from AGN that OKH had authorised, its commander was criticised for not retaining any bridgeheads to enable counter-attacks. Indeed, there were still German troops east of the Western Dvina but no bridges remained intact. However, the major problem facing Third Panzer Army's leader, General Reinhardt, was the gap between VI AC and LIII AC as VI AC's left flank was hanging in the air, as was the right of LIII AC. It was impossible to fill this gap as there were no forces available. Reinhardt, well aware of the *Feste Platz* doctrine, nevertheless requested the city and its defenders be evacuated. It was a situation in which every hour counted as the momentum of the Soviet advance to the north of Vitebsk was increasing alarmingly. At 1535hrs that afternoon Reinhardt was informed that Hitler had decided that Vitebsk was to be held as a 'fortress, and that everything must be attempted so the formations can hold it'. Busch contributed the thought that one division should be sufficient to hold Vitebsk. The designated unit was 206th Infantry Division and, in accordance with Führer Order 11, its commander, *Generalleutnant* Hitter, became Commander of Fortress Vitebsk at 0400hrs on 25 June. The other divisions were granted permission to break out to the west led by the commander of LIII AC, General Gollwitzer. At 1315hrs Hitter reported that Vitebsk was now surrounded, that LIII AC's 6th LFD and 246th Infantry Division were heavily engaged, as was 4th LFD. The likelihood of Vitebsk holding out was marginal as street fighting raged in suburban areas throughout the night of 25–26 June. At almost the same time, AGC's Chief of Staff received a message from OKH that Hitler expected Vitebsk to hold out for another week. Simultaneously, units of Third Panzer Army were being redistributed; VI AC transferred to Fourth Army while IX AC, north of the Western Dvina River line, went to AGN's Sixteenth Army. This latter transfer included three precious assault gun brigades. In effect, Third Panzer Army was being disassembled by both Soviet attacks and AGC/OKH's responses.

As its War Diary entry for 25 June had laconically noted, 'During today, the position of the Third Panzer Army became worse every hour.'

With the bulk of LIII AC now effectively surrounded in and around Vitebsk, its breakout may have looked feasible on paper, however the situation on the ground was very different due to the speed of the Soviet advance and the inability of German intelligence to keep abreast of developments. Late on 25 June, the division assigned to spearhead the breakout, 4th LFD, had been destroyed by Third Belarusian Front's Thirty-Ninth Army, while the other two breakout divisions, 6th LFD and 246th Infantry, were both threatened with a similar fate. The transfer of the StuG III brigades had reduced the anti-tank capability of the Third Panzer Army to little more than mines and hand-held weapons such as the *Panzerfaust*. Taking into account that Vitebsk was to be held by an infantry division, the redeployment of the mobile anti-tank weapons, mainly StuG III assault guns, made sense as the experience of Stalingrad had demonstrated that armour was wasted in an urban combat environment. Better to preserve such assets for counter-attacks to relieve the beleaguered city's garrison.

However, events had moved so much more rapidly than anticipated that 206th Infantry Division was isolated and was itself breaking up as Soviet troops moved into the city itself despite the destruction of almost all the river bridges.

Meanwhile, the breakout force, now including elements of 206th Infantry Division, along with Hitter (the garrison commander himself) and Gollwitzer, LIII AC's commander, began its move south-westwards. Things went wrong from the outset. The dump of supplies assigned to the escaping units was destroyed by Soviet air strikes. Gollwitzer requested supplies be air dropped but, given Soviet dominance of the skies, this measure was never seriously considered at AGC's HQ. Nor was LIII AC aware that Third Belarusian Front had ordered its Cavalry-Mechanised Group, consisting of III Guards Cavalry and III Guards Mechanised corps, forward to exploit the gaps now that the German defence lines had been breached. This group included large numbers of cavalry and up to 140 tanks that were tasked with rapid advances to cause havoc, keeping the enemy off balance and seizing bridgeheads and vulnerable targets before defensive positions could be established. Furthermore, the German breakout forces had undergone a series of Soviet attacks that had damaged their cohesion and they were now split into two large groups.

Despite these problems, the Germans had managed to mount a number of counter-attacks against the still fragile Soviet line, but as more and more Red Army men arrived, their positions firmed up. Indeed, had the men of LIII AC but known it, such was the void behind the opposition's encirclement that they would have to cover roughly 80km to reach anything resembling friendly positions.

At 0345hrs Gollwitzer sent his last radio message in which he swore, 'I take a personal oath to fight to the end.' He informed Third Panzer Army's HQ that the enemy line had been penetrated and that his men required air cover. Soviet jamming precluded any further radio contact. Gollwitzer's last appeal to his men was, 'Force this breakthrough, you must not let your general down!'

According to some Soviet sources, the German attacks were mounted without concern, almost suicidal in nature and many of the attackers were drunk. Hundreds of German troops were killed or wounded until senior officers managed to regain control of the almost anarchic situation. Now broken down into smaller units, many Germans took advantage of the summer night to slip quietly through enemy lines. Elsewhere, other breakout units enacted similar scenes. As dawn broke over LIII AC on 27 June, the Soviets called for the unconditional surrender of the Vitebsk garrison and other pockets of resistance in the area, which was accepted. Gollwitzer and Hitter, along with many other senior officers, went into captivity. The commanders of the two LFD, Generals Peschel and Pistorius, were both killed in action. The Soviet figures give 20,000 Germans killed and 10,000 captured. However, what had taken both OKH and AGC completely by surprise was the ferocity, power and unparalleled efficiency of the Red Army's operation. The apparent ease and speed with which German defence lines had been broken was totally unexpected. Additionally, there was now little in the way to challenge further Soviet advances towards the Berezina River, which was the next major water barrier behind which to create a defence line as it ran roughly north to south-east of Minsk. Little, if anything, had been done to entrench this potential barrier due to Hitler's attitude towards, as he put it, generals who looked backwards and favoured flexible defence tactics that involved surrendering ground. Unsurprisingly, Busch had not encouraged his deputies to even plan such a line. Equally worrying was the disruption of the connection of AGC's left flank with the right of AGN.

Now, with Second Belarusian and First Belarusian (right wing only) fronts engaged along the rest of AGC's Belarusian Balcony, it was clear that Stavka was not bluffing about its intentions towards AGC. But *Feste Platz* Vitebsk and Third Panzer Army were only part of the picture, Fourth Army and *Festung* (fortress) Orsha were also being subjected to Stalin's hammer.

The destruction of a bridge by an unidentified partisan unit during the night of 19 June. Although the waterway looks narrow, the banks were frequently marshy and extended for many dozens of metres beyond the river's course. The partisans were credited with the construction of 312 bridges and crossing points during Operation Bagration. The majority of these were submerged and unobserved by the Germans. (*Courtesy of the Central Museum of the Armed Forces, Moscow via Stavka*)

Attached to AGC's rear area security forces was a potpourri of units including Cossack collaborators such as these. As cavalry they were a more mobile and capable anti-partisan force than the ordinary German security troops. With a reputation for ruthlessness, they proved adept when fighting irregular forces. However, they were less useful when fighting Red Army veterans in a front-line role. (*Nik Cornish at www.stavka.photos*)

As the number of partisan raids on the essential rail links behind AGC increased, so security at stations was stepped up. Local railway employees were targeted by the partisans and those who would not support them were often shot out of hand. The Germans frequently took rail workers' families hostage to ensure their cooperation. Further measures included the clearance of trees and undergrowth to a depth of 100–200m to provide clear lines of sight. According to the Head of the Transport Department of AGC, this partisan operation caused, 'a complete halt to railway traffic on all important communications leading to the breakthrough sites'. (*Nik Cornish at www.stavka.photos*)

Equally difficult to secure were roads and bridges. The major paved road running from Moscow to Minsk was a vital part of AGC's transport web. Here a British-made Scammel Pioneer lorry tows a trailer of Germans and repair kit to secure a bridge damaged by partisans. Local workers, mainly female, have been impressed as labourers. (*Nik Cornish at www.stavka.photos*)

At 0500hrs, Moscow time, on 22 June a twenty-minute barrage heralded the reconnaissance in force phase of Operation Bagration on Third Baltic Front's zone. This well-camouflaged 152mm M. 1937 howitzer is about to fire. It had a range of just over 17km. (*Courtesy of the Central Museum of the Armed Forces, Moscow via Stavka*)

Nor was it only Soviet artillery that pounded German positions. The Soviet Air Force (VVS) flew hundreds of sorties targeting artillery positions, troop concentrations, supply lines and fortified areas. Here an Il-2 Shturmovik prepares to leave a forward airfield. The 78th Sturm Division's HQ had been the subject of such an attack. (*Courtesy of the Central Museum of the Armed Forces, Moscow via Stavka*)

Luftflotte 6, responsible for the air support for AGC, was almost powerless in the face of the numbers of Soviet aircraft and the hugely improved tactical use of the VVS. Lacking fuel, and with the defence of the Reich now the priority, air superiority for the Luftwaffe over the Eastern Front was long past. (*Nik Cornish at www.stavka.photos*)

Fourth Army's defences east of the Dnepr River from Orsha were relatively strong, having held off a series of Soviet attacks earlier in the year. However, the bombardment, both by artillery and from the air, had degraded them somewhat. Here German infantry trying to clear debris from their positions are not helped by unseasonal downpours of rain. Their fall back line was west of the Dnepr. (*Nik Cornish at www.stavka.photos*)

Mines were a vital part of the German defensive system, particularly in the approaches to the Minsk highway. To counter this threat, Third Belarusian Front deployed the PT-34 mine roller. These specialised machines were deployed in Separate Engineering Tank Regiments. (*Nik Cornish at www.stavka.photos*)

To keep the pressure on the Germans, Soviet infantry were carried along in pursuit on the sides of tanks, as seen here. T-34s were provided with grip rails on their turrets to enable their passengers some degree of security. (*From the fonds of the RGAKFD in Krasnogorsk via Stavka*)

AGC's infantry, having fought a semi-static form of defensive warfare for several months and lacking transport, were finding themselves more and more isolated and less aware of the whereabouts of their parent units and the enemy. Morale began to decay, especially in the newer formations. (*Nik Cornish at www.stavka.photos*)

A fifth of Third Panzer Army's LIII AC infantry was made up of Luftwaffe ground crew. Raised in mid-1942 to provide manpower, the Luftwaffe Field Divisions were poor relations in terms of experience, training and equipment to their Heer (Army) counterparts. The 4th LFD was to have spearheaded the breakout from Vitebsk but was outclassed, surrounded and wiped out by its Red Army opposition. (*Nik Cornish at www.stavka.photos*)

All types of mines and booby traps were sown across the path of the Soviet advance. Here a Red Army engineer tests the ground with a simple probe. In his hands are a pair of wire cutters. *(Courtesy of the Central Museum of the Armed Forces, Moscow via Stavka)*

A partisan patrol makes its way along a newly laid corduroy road to meet up with an advancing Red Army unit. The partisans' local knowledge and forest lore was to prove invaluable during Operation Bagration. (*Nik Cornish at www.stavka.photos*)

Street fighting in Vitebsk city centre. Soviet troops advance towards a fortified boys' school. *(Courtesy of the Central Museum of the Armed Forces, Moscow via Stavka)*

Soviet infantry celebrate the liberation of Vitebsk. On 26 June Senior Sergeant Blokhin and his engineers rushed a group of German troops and managed to cut the fuse preventing the destruction of this bridge over the Western Dvina River. He was awarded the order of Hero of the Soviet Union, the highest accolade in the Red Army, and the bridge was renamed in his honour. *(Courtesy of the Central Museum of the Armed Forces, Moscow via Stavka)*

Both before and during Operation Bagration, traffic control was essential due to the poor road network and the number of vehicles moving forwards. The majority of traffic control personnel were female. The problem of fresh drinking water was eased by the provision of water stations, such as that on the left signposted 'Boiling Water'. (*Courtesy of the Central Museum of the Armed Forces, Moscow via Stavka*)

During the early days of Operation Bagration the crew of an M1910 Maxim machine gun struggle out of one of many of the many tributaries that fed into the Dnepr and Western Dvina rivers. *(Courtesy of the Central Museum of the Armed Forces, Moscow via Stavka)*

German POWs march through Vitebsk. Despite the offer of surrender, many German troops fought to the end as there was a widespread fear of capture due to propaganda and rumours of the fate of those who fell into Soviet captivity. (*Courtesy of the Central Museum of the Armed Forces, Moscow via Stavka*)

Chapter Three

Festung Orsha

Feste Platz Orsha was situated mainly on the right bank of the Dnepr River at its confluence with the Orshitsa River. Its location as a bridging point across the Dnepr, being the junction of four major rail lines and its proximity to the Moscow–Minsk highway, all contributed to its importance as part of the German defensive network for Belarus. When Bagration began, Orsha was some 25km behind the front line. Tippelskirch's Fourth Army, defending the line from the right flank of Third Panzer Army, some 30km north of Orsha, consisted of XXVII, XXXIX Panzer and XII AC, which adjoined Ninth Army's left flank, south of Mogilev. The strongest of the XXVII AC's units, 78th 'Sturm' Division, defended the highway to Minsk with 25th Panzer Grenadier Division on its right flank. The remainder of Fourth Army's line was held by several understrength infantry divisions. Its reserves consisted of 286th Security Division and the twenty Tiger I tanks, half of its establishment strength, of Heavy Tank Battalion 501. The balance of the Tiger battalion's machines had been moved to AGNU, while their crews had gone to the rear for training on the new Tiger II. As well as this, albeit small, armoured formation, Fourth Army was well-provided with StuG III assault guns. The two divisions noted earlier fielded thirty-one and forty-five respectively. Each of the other infantry divisions listed between six and ten StuG IIIs. XII AC 18th Panzer Grenadier Division included forty-three StuG IIIs. Another unit, Panzer Grenadier Division *Feldherrnhalle*, was also in the area but was part of AGC's reserve and therefore only to be committed to action when Busch permitted. *Feldherrnhalle* was itself a strong division that could deploy both tanks and assault guns.

Across the Dnepr from Fourth Army were Third and Second Belarusian fronts. Directly facing the Minsk highway were Third Belarusian Front's Eleventh Guards and Thirty-First Armies. According to Stavka's orders of 31 May, these units would, 'attack along the Minsk highway in the general direction of Borisov [a bridging point over the Berezina River east of Minsk]; part of [this] group to capture the city of Orsha from the north. The attack would then develop towards Borisov in cooperation with the Second Belarusian Front, to defeat the enemy's Borisov group and reach the western bank of the Berezina River.' Once the German defences had been breached, mobile exploitation would be carried out by the II Guards Tank Corps.

The Third Belarusian Front's offensive was scheduled to start on 23 June but such was the success achieved in the direction of Vitebsk that it began twenty-four hours earlier.

The infantry attacked at 0900hrs. Krylov's Fifth Army focussed on the right flank, LXXII AC and LXV AC striking German VI AC and advancing some 10km during the course of the day. As this was happening, Thirty-Ninth Army's V Guards Rifle Corps cut the Vitebsk–Orsha railway line and captured three crossing points on the Luchesa River that formed part of the German defences north of Orsha. A railway bridge across the same river fell to units of Fifth Army further to the south. Naturally, a series of increasingly desperate counter-attacks were launched but all failed to regain these strategic assets. Eleventh Army made less progress against more solid resistance, as did Thirty-First Army south of Orsha.

Tippelskirch, recognising the power of the Soviet offensive and his need for a shortened line to create a reserve, requested permission to pull his troops back across the Dnepr. Busch's eventual response was allow Panzer Grenadier Division *Feldherrnhalle* to move into covering positions along the Dnepr's western bank. When *Generalmajor* Steinkeller, commanding *Feldherrnhalle*, reported to XXXIX Panzer Corps' commander *Generalleutnant* Martinek, Martinek apparently said, 'What kind of breakthrough should you close? We have nothing but continuous breakthroughs here. Your place is on the Berezina to provide a reserve line of defence there in case we cannot hold on the Dnepr. And this will happen pretty soon.' Steinkeller's response is unavailable.

By the morning of 24 June Fourth Army was almost stretched to breaking point, a situation Busch recognised by agreeing to allow its left wing to fall back some 8km. However, he rejected a request to shorten the line facing Thirty-First Army and Second Belarusian Front's Thirty-Third army by withdrawing to the Dnepr with the comment, 'The prepared positions may not be abandoned because the enemy would receive encouragement.' Encouragement was not something the Red Army required. As 78th Sturm Division pulled back, so too did 12th and 337th Infantry Divisions south of Orsha, where they covered it and the northern approaches to *Festung* Mogilev. Withdrawing under pressure led to a gap forming between these two divisions. A further gap, between 78th Sturm Division and Third Panzer Army's 256th Infantry Division on its left, where the ground was wet and swampy, had also appeared. Tippelskirch had nothing close enough to plug either hole in his line. Nevertheless, Fourth Army was still in reasonably good shape as seven out of ten of its divisions remained combat worthy. Indeed, 78th Sturm and 25th Panzer Grenadier Divisions were holding Eleventh Guards Army, denying it the breakthroughs achieved elsewhere. And then, in the early hours of 25 June, AGC HQ informed Fourth Army that, '120 Soviet tanks had broken through at the village of Bogushevsk in VI AC zone of defence'. Bogushevsk was roughly halfway between Orsha and Vitebsk. Later that day VI AC became Fourth Army's responsibility. The day's good news for Busch and Tippelskirch was the release by OKH of 5th Panzer Division, which would be sent by rail to reinforce AGC from AGNU. Slowly the seriousness of the assault on AGC was becoming apparent at Führer HQ. However, the questions of how long this reinforcement would take to arrive and where to deploy it when it did remained moot. Partisan activity along the railways to AGC's rear continued and the situation AGC was in found itself changing almost hourly. The other problem was where were the '120 Soviet tanks' of Third Belarusian Front's Cavalry-Mechanised Group, for such they were, going? Tippelskirch had already committed the Tigers of Heavy Tank Battalion 501 north-east of

Orsha on 23 June, where they had been involved in furious armour-on-armour combat. Heavy Tank Battalion 501 was now short of ammunition and fuel and had lost at least one Tiger when a bridge collapsed under its weight, thus further slowing the redeployment.

To counter the threat of the Cavalry-Mechanised Group heading to the south-west, Tippelskirch ordered XXVII AC, in front of Orsha itself, to concentrate all of its assault guns and self-propelled artillery on its left wing to contain this Soviet armoured force.

By 25 June Fourth Army's situation had reached crisis point. Communications between Tippelskirch's HQ and Busch's AGC HQ and Busch with Führer HQ were taking more time to resolve questions than the Red Army was taking to raise them, such was the speed of the advance. Unbeknownst to the Germans, Fifth Guards Tank Army, which had now been committed to the exploitation phase of the offensive, was in the process of changing positions to support Fifth Army's breakthrough. Simultaneously, Eleventh Guards Army was grinding its way through the stubbornly held defences of 78th Assault Division above Orsha as XXVII AC gave ground. Similar situations were developing elsewhere along Fourth Army's front. Panzer Grenadier Division *Feldherrnhalle*, to the south, reported Soviet breakthroughs in that area towards Mogilev, which raised the threat of the encirclement of Fourth Army in its entirety. Consequently, Tippelskirch decided to take matters into his own hands and withdrew all units north of Orsha back to the Dnepr River. When Busch discovered what was going on he informed Tippelskirch that this was 'an act in contravention of orders' and that he should reverse these movements. XXXIX Panzer and XXVII AC, south and east of Orsha respectively, were ordered by Tippelskirch to 'hold firm until they are attacked by a superior enemy force and then pushed back. The only troops to be withdrawn are those needed to cover the gap between 78th Assault and 25th Panzer Grenadier divisions and those needed to cover the Dnepr crossings that are threatened.' He had not obeyed Busch's order for lesser withdrawals. Happily for Tippelskirch there was no time for further discussion as Hitler then approved Tippelskirch's orders at 2310hrs that night. Unfortunately for Fourth Army, it was too little too late to have any significant effect.

At 0820hrs AGC's Chief of Staff, *Generalleutnant* Hans Krebs, informed Fourth Army that there was now a 50km gap between themselves and Third Panzer Army. Into this Soviet tanks, armour and infantry were moving and it was impossible to fill the hole. Krebs added the further bad news that LIII AC had failed to either hold its positions or break out and that Fourth Army must surrender an assault gun brigade, in theory twenty-eight vehicles, for Army Group use.

Meanwhile, VI AC, which had been out of contact with Tippelskirch for several hours, restored communications with yet more bad news. Its 256th Infantry Division had been surrounded and its commander killed. Fourth Army HQ responded by ordering VI AC to send some Tiger Is of Heavy Tank Battalion 501 to Tolotschin, roughly 55km west of Orsha and close to the Moscow–Minsk highway, in an attempt to establish contact with Third Panzer Army's right flank and some form of blocking position. By this time XXVII AC was under continual pressure as it fell back westwards to the Orsha bridgehead over the Dnepr River. That afternoon, despite requests to cancel Orsha's *Feste Platz* designation, *Generalleutnant* Traut, commanding 78th Assault Division, was appointed its Commandant. As he took on his new role, Traut was unaware that II Guards Tank Corps had passed north of the city, detaching a tank brigade to complete its encirclement from the west. However, he was somewhat confused as he had been given permission to withdraw by XXVII AC as the city was under threat from Fifth and Eleventh Guards Armies from the north and elements of Thirty-First Army from the south. Indeed, XXXVI Guards Rifle Corps (Eleventh Army) was already engaging his men in heavy street fighting. Therefore, Traut reasoned, he was unable to deploy his forces to effectively hold *Festung* Orsha. By his interpretation of Führer Order 11, Traut was therefore unable to carry out orders and it was permissible to save his division from complete destruction by withdrawal.

As the Soviets described it, 'At 1820hrs on June 26, the assault on the city began, and by 2300hrs street fighting began. The enemy turned stone buildings into powerful nodes of resistance, and set up long-term firing points at all road crossings. 152-mm howitzers and combat vehicles of the 517th Flamethrower Tank Regiment were used to destroy and suppress them. By 0900 on 27 June, the formations of both armies had completely captured the city. They captured nine railway trains, 15 steam locomotives, 1,250 wagons, 37 guns, 19 tanks and armoured vehicles, 161 tractors, 1,950 motor vehicles and tractors, 23 different warehouses, as well as other weapons and equipment. The enemy lost 1,200 killed and more than 100 soldiers and officers captured.' Although Traut and many of the 'garrison' had managed to leave, their escape route would be fraught with difficulty.

In XXXIX AC's zone, despite parts of the Dnepr line holding, units of Forty-Ninth Army had crossed the river and was driving elements of Panzer Grenadier Division *Feldherrnhalle* back from their positions north of Mogilev, placing its entire position in danger of collapse. Steinkeller later commented, 'I managed, more by luck than skilful command, to transport my troops back across the Dnepr at Mogilev.' Once again Tippelskirch requested permission from AGN HQ to pull back but Krebs was unable to do so, nor would he take the responsibility for such a move while Busch was absent. Busch had flown to report AGC's situation in person to the Führer. Remarkably, Hitler granted permission to pull Fourth Army back to the Berezina River in stages: he still insisted that *Feste Platz* Orsha and Mogilev be held. However, the fall of Orsha led to both Eleventh and Thirty-First Soviet Armies opening up their field of attack along their entire frontage.

Defending the Moscow–Minsk highway was one of Fourth Army's major priorities. The crew of this heavily camouflaged 88mm gun are positioned to cover the highway but are deployed to provide air defence. Judging by the 'kill' rings, they seem to have enjoyed a successful war. *(Nik Cornish at www.stavka.photos)*

Viewed from the hull top of a command machine, several SU-152, nicknamed 'animal killers' due to their ability to destroy Elefants, Tigers and Panthers, move towards Fourth Army positions. One drawback was the lack of ammunition storage, 20 rounds only, which led the crews to carry more ammunition on the engine decks. These heavy self-propelled guns were usually attached to rifle divisions. *(Courtesy of the Central Museum of the Armed Forces, Moscow via Stavka)*

An SdKfz 164 'Nashorn' (renamed Hornisse) self-propelled anti-tank gun, one of 18 deployed by 78th Sturm Division during June 1944. The 88mm gun was capable of destroying almost all Soviet tanks. (*Nik Cornish at www.stavka.photos*)

By coincidence, it was near Orsha in 1941 that the Red Army first used Katyusha rocket launchers in action. Three years later this upgraded, battle-proven weapons system was used once again. This is a BM-13 132mm launcher mounted on a Lend-Lease Studebaker truck. (*From the fonds of the RGAKFD in Krasnogorsk via Stavka*)

The Soviet artillery preparation directed at Fourth Army was a sophisticated exercise in destruction that targeted each line of defence, in order, with varying degrees of intensity. After a specified period, in the case of the initial bombardment some 170 minutes, three further minutes of firing was allowed before the infantry went over the top. As the infantry advanced, the shelling was directed at defences deeper in the German line. (*Courtesy of the Central Museum of the Armed Forces, Moscow via Stavka*)

Despite discouragement from Hitler and other problems, some areas of AGC's line, particularly covering the Minsk highway, included some strong positions. Here a Soviet BT-7 tank, probably captured during 1941, has been dug in to provide some anti-tank gun cover. (*Nik Cornish at www.stavka.photos*)

When it became clear to the local population that the Soviet offensive was going well, thousands of people turned themselves into partisans and went 'Fritz Hunting'. German stragglers, singly or in small groups, often from rear-echelon units proved to be easy targets for mobs of civilians bent on revenge and eager to prove their loyalty to the Soviet state. (*Courtesy of the Central Museum of the Armed Forces, Moscow via Stavka*)

During the early hours of Third Belarusian Front's probing attacks, Fifth Army units recorded that they 'repelled counter-attacks (and) defeated 550th Penal Battalion ...' The 500 series of German units were manned by troops undergoing probationary service for various misdemeanours. It was not unknown for them to defect to the Red Army as such battalions were usually deployed at critical points of the front. (*Courtesy of the Central Museum of the Armed Forces, Moscow via Stavka*)

Feldherrnhalle Panzer Grenadier Division could deploy seventeen Panzer IV, such as those here, and seventeen StuG III assault guns. Substantial camouflage was vital due to the Soviets control of the skies. The 75mm gun was able to penetrate the armour of most Soviet tanks depending on the range. It is interesting to note that AGC had no Panzer V Panthers at its disposal. (*Nik Cornish at www.stavka.photos*)

Led by a T-34, infantry of Second Belarusian Front cross one of several tributaries of the Dnepr River. AGC was blessed with many defensible water courses but was unable to create substantial positions due to Hitler's suspicion of officers who proposed such things and regarded them as 'looking too often to the rear'. (*Courtesy of the Central Museum of the Armed Forces, Moscow via Stavka*)

Despite the low cloud and rain on 24 June, eighteen Il-2s attacked the HQ of 78th Sturm Division. Later that day 162 Pe-2 light bombers, as seen here, struck at positions in front of Eleventh Guards Army. The Pe-2 was capable of carrying 1,000kg of bombs. (*Courtesy of the Central Museum of the Armed Forces, Moscow via Stavka*)

When the Germans began to fall back, their rate of movement was slowed due to so much of the transport being horse drawn, the condition of the roads and the numerous streams and rivers to be crossed. (*Nik Cornish at www.stavka.photos*)

An OT-34 flamethrower tank of the type employed by the 517th Flamethrower Tank Regiment during the street fighting in Orsha. The flamethrower replaced the hull machine gun and had a range of up to 65m. (*From the fonds of the RGAKFD in Krasnogorsk via Stavka*)

The defences on the eastern bank of the Dnepr River, opposite Orsha, were solidly built and served their purpose well until threatened with outflanking thrusts to the north and south. Here a group of German troops takes a quick meal. (*Nik Cornish at www.stavka.photos*)

A well-prepared and cleverly camouflaged German mortar position, with its spotter to the left behind the reed screen, prepares to fire. (*Nik Cornish at www.stavka.photos*)

Off-road almost anywhere in the path of Operation Bagration was terrain to break the heart of tank troops. The vehicle commanders of these T-34s need to spot for their drivers in an attempt to avoid any problems ahead. Clearly by doing this they are ideal targets for any German snipers. The ensuing hold-up would render the entire column prey to tank-hunting teams. (*Courtesy of the Central Museum of the Armed Forces, Moscow via Stavka*)

A Soviet infantry section moves cautiously through marshy woodland. Whatever had been said to the ordinary Ivan before the start of Operation Bagration, the German Army still had a reputation for tenacious defence. For those Red army men brought up in more urban environments, the Belarusian countryside resembled a jungle. (*Courtesy of the Central Museum of the Armed Forces, Moscow via Stavka*)

Dozens of German POWs await orders to march off. One Soviet veteran recalled, 'They would wait for the order to "march off" and then leave in a disciplined fashion. Along the way stragglers, alone or in groups, would leave their hiding places and join them. Clearly happier to be in the hands of the Red Army than those of the partisans.' (*Courtesy of the Central Museum of the Armed Forces, Moscow via Stavka*)

Chapter Four

Festung Mogilev

Mogilev was known throughout the USSR as the last HQ of the last Tsar of Russia, Nicholas II, which he left in March 1917 to abdicate in the wake of the revolution. Before its occupation by the Germans, in July 1941, it had a population of some 100,000 people, of whom roughly 20 per cent were Jewish. By 1943, along with the bulk of towns in Belarus, the majority of the Jews were corralled in the local ghetto and murdered as part of Hitler's ethnic cleansing plans. A further 30,000 civilians of Belarusian and Russian extraction were sent as 'volunteer' workers to Germany.

During the advance through Belarus in 1941, AGC had been held up around Mogilev and forced into besieging the city. The defence of Mogilev slowed the advance eastwards by almost three weeks due to the stubborn resistance of its defenders and the railway bridge was destroyed by Red Army engineers. Finally, on 27 July, as the last pockets of defenders were overrun, the Soviet commander decided, against orders, to break out of the encirclement.

By the spring of 1944 Mogilev's position as a bridging point, for both road and rail, over the Dnepr River again made it a target of strategic importance, this time to the Red Army, and a series of operations were launched by Western Front to take it and break through Fourth Army's right flank. None of these efforts achieved their objectives. As a result of Western Front's failure, Stavka launched an enquiry, mentioned in Chapter One, that concluded, 'All these operations ended unsuccessfully … the operation ended, at best, with an insignificant wedge [being driven] into the enemy's defence with large losses to our troops.' As a result, the Front commander, its heads of intelligence and artillery were all reassigned.

However, as with other failures in this region at the same time, vital lessons were learnt and, more significantly, acted upon. It is important to note that these lessons, so bloodily taught, were also applied across the Fronts that would be participating in Operation Bagration. Stavka's investigative commission noted four areas of major concern:

1. The offensive command underestimated the strength and depth of German defences and the added advantages they enjoyed such as the geological factor that Russian riverbanks on the western side overlooked the flatter, lower eastern shore.

2. Inadequate artillery preparation, particularly in terms of locating and supressing enemy batteries, which were able to halt infantry attacks and inflict heavy losses on them.
3. Poor training and front-line leadership. 'Untrained units and officers did not make any manoeuvres on the battlefield but lay down under enemy fire and allowed themselves to be destroyed ... losses in manpower were mainly from artillery fire.'
4. Poor use of armour. 'The command of the Western Front threw II Guards Tank Corps against the undefeated enemy defences, as a result of which the corps could not advance and suffered heavy losses.

In view of this report it is scarcely any wonder that the new commander of Second Belarusian Front, as Western Front was renamed, Colonel General G. F. Zakharov, was at great pains to ensure these issues were addressed rapidly. As Second Belarusian Front's Thirty-Third Army was to act mainly in support of Third Belarusian Front's left flank, it was left to Zakharov's two remaining armies, Forty-Ninth, facing Mogilev, and Fiftieth to its left at the junction with First Belarusian Front, to accomplish what Western Front had signally failed to achieve.

Of all the Fronts involved in Operation Bagration, Second Belarusian Front was the weakest, certainly in terms of armour. It fielded only 276 tanks and armoured fighting vehicles organised into two brigades, 42nd and 43rd Guards Tank Brigades in Forty-Ninth Army. This was because, as the Front Co-ordinator Marshal Zhukov, pointed out, 'there was no point in pushing the enemy out of Mogilev until ... First and Third Belarusian fronts reached the deep rear of ... AGC'. These were the main forces in the early part of Bagration and contained the largest armoured and mobile formations. Furthermore, the roads and terrain facing Zakharov's forces were particularly unsuited for mechanised warfare. It was also sensible to consider the possibility that the Soviet breakthrough would succeed all along the Front's lines and therefore one of the last things that Stavka wanted was an immense traffic jam that proved unmanageable and thus presented even a depleted Luftwaffe with a wonderful target. Stavka was aiming for the total destruction of AGC, not merely its partial defeat.

Therefore, to allow First and Third Belarusian Fronts to push ahead and give Second Belarusian Front room to operate, its start date for the offensive was 23 June.

Zakharov had chosen Forty-Ninth Army to spearhead the attack. Led by Lieutenant General I. T. Grishin, its four Rifle Corps would attack along a 12km front that ran along the Pronya River. From there it would cross the Basia River and several lesser waterways followed by the Dnepr River itself and then liberate Mogilev. This was all to be accomplished by the fifth day of the operation. Support on Forty-Ninth Army's left flank would be provided by the right flanking units of Fiftieth Army.

Facing Second Belarusian Front were XXXIX Panzer and XII AC. The former had no tanks but did include fifty-eight StuG IIIs, while XII AC's two infantry divisions, 57th and 267th, had fifteen StuG IIIs between them. Due to Fourth Army's defensive achievements earlier in the year, this force was deemed sufficient to hold off any repeat performance by the, so the Germans believed, tactically unsophisticated Red Army. Three lines of defence protected Mogilev and the Dnepr River crossings that included fortified villages, minefields and solidly built trench systems and firing positions.

As the guns rumbled ominously to the north, the German front-line troops along the Pronya River did not sleep easy wondering how long it would be before it was their turn to be under Soviet fire. Their turn was not slow in coming. At 0400hrs on 22 June the usual reconnaissance in force began following hard on the heels of a thirty-minute barrage. With the Soviet artillery keeping German heads well down, a scout patrol of 330th Rifle Division managed to cross the Pronya River, proving the feasibility and value of closely following the shelling. But despite small incursions, Soviet gains were minor. However, what came the next day demonstrated to AGC that the Red Army's artillery had learnt from its previous mistakes. Postponed due to bad weather from 0500hrs to 0900hrs (Moscow time, two hours ahead of the Berlin time that the Germans kept) the main attack began with a two-hour bombardment.

A German POW later told his interrogators, 'On the morning of 23 June hurricane fire began. The shells mixed everything into the ground. The trenches were obliterated. When, two hours later, the Russians had already bypassed us. We were surrounded and resistance was impossible.' In 331st Rifle Division's sector the Soviets advanced 6km, and during the course of the day other breakthroughs were made in XXXIX AC's front line. Under fire, Forty-Ninth Army's combat engineers had managed to put in place a bridge with sixty tons capacity, more than enough to cope with the T-34. Elsewhere along the Pronya River, dozens of smaller crossing points had been established by infantrymen who managed to extemporise methods of getting across the water.

Obviously such potential bridgeheads swiftly became the focus of German artillery and counter-attacks but in most cases the lack of Luftwaffe or armoured support (this was true for both sides) meant that they made little headway. Hand-to-hand fighting was the nature of much of the first day's combat. Nevertheless, Forty-Ninth Army had, by nightfall, penetrated German defences across a front of over 15km to a depth of 8km.

Although Zakharov did not know it, Tippelskirch was sufficiently concerned with Forty-Ninth Army's progress and the fact that his men were now being stretched to their limit that he had requested permission to withdraw to the covering positions on the eastern bank of the Dnepr River. Inevitably his request was denied. However, the Germans' failure to regain their forward positions and increasing Soviet pressure inexorably forced 12th and the severely weakened 337th Infantry Divisions back towards their second line along the Basia River. However, as this movement was under way, a gap started to form between them which it was impossible to fill due to a lack of manpower and the demands on Fourth Army further north around Orsha. Soviet forward units passed this information back to the HQ and, in order to prevent the Germans regrouping along the Basia, a mobile force was cobbled together and rushed forward. Such was the confusion at XXXIX Panzer Corps' HQ that lorry-borne Soviet infantry were able to cross the Basia at four points; luckily for Fourth Army these incursions were just contained before they made further progress towards the Dnepr. However, Forty-Ninth Army did not rest on its laurels and began to move supporting forces to help reinforce the bridgeheads.

Elsewhere, Fiftieth Army had not been idle and, building on the inexorable pressure that Forty-Ninth Army was exerting crossed the Pronya, and, pushing the defenders back steadily, liberated the regional centre of the Mogilev District, Chausy, on 25 June. The news that this administrative centre had been freed led to a, '20 salvo 224 gun salute' being fired in Moscow to celebrate, 'the valiant troops of Second Belarusian Front who crossed the Pronya River'.

With all eyes now on Forty-Ninth Army as it prepared to force the Basia in strength, Tippelskirch had been permitted to commit his reserve unit, parts of the Panzer Grenadier Division *Feldhernnhalle*, into supporting positions along the Basia. However, as some sub-units of this formation had been employed elsewhere, it was not as strong as it appeared on paper. When Forty-Ninth Army began its next push, at 0600hrs on 25 June, it was preceded by yet another powerful artillery and aerial assault. Seven rifle divisions went into the attack and crossed the Basia where, despite the, by now, disjointed and understrength counter-attacks, several solid bridgeheads were established. Later that evening, as noted in Chapter Three, Tippelskirch ordered XXXIX AC back to the Dnepr covering positions.

As Forty-Ninth Army moved troops forward and realigned its positions during the night of 25–26 June, Zakharov, wishing to increase the momentum of his Front's advance and, under pressure from Stavka via Marshall Zhukov to increase the pace of his Front's relatively tardy advance, passed the pressure on to his subordinates. He therefore ordered Thirty-Third Army back into the fray to attack, across its entire frontage, facing what remained of 337th Infantry Division, parts of Panzer Grenadier Division *Feldhernnhalle* and elements of 110th Infantry Division. On Second Belarusian Front's left flank, Fiftieth Army was to employ its more mobile units to reach the eastern bank of the Dnepr, south-east of Mogilev. At the same time, Forty-Ninth Army, the Front's main assault force, was to use two rifle corps in support of its advance units to reach the Dnepr's eastern bank north of Mogilev by the end of 26 June. The Forty-Ninth Army's mobile force was to have crossed the Dnepr ahead of the rifle corps by that time.

With their orders clear and uncompromising, the Soviet formations made their preparations as their engineers worked around the clock to improve the tracks leading to the river crossings for vehicles. Staff officers rushed hither and thither to ensure the traffic jams were sorted out, prioritising those units that were essential to the advance, be they tanks, fuel or munitions. Happily, the weather was improving and the ground drying out. This enabled Fourth Air Army to increase the amount of support it could provide by operating, virtually unopposed, strafing and bombing raids on German columns and positions. Such attacks, on XXXIX Panzer Corps, played a significant role in its loss of cohesion that night. Its 12th, 31st and 110th Infantry Divisions were gradually breaking up as they struggled to pull back to the apparent safety of the Dnepr River. In fact, parts of 110th Infantry Division had fallen in with XXVII AC, while the rest of it was only in radio contact with its parent corps' HQ by radio and that was increasingly subject to jamming.

On the afternoon of 26 June, XII AC's commander, *Generalleutnant* Vincenz Müller, is alleged to have lost his head and issued the order, 'Troops push through to the west! Divisions are dismissed', which caused a considerable degree of confusion across Fourth Army. Recognising this order as potentially disastrous for Fourth Army, Steinkeller decided that his command, Panzer Grenadier Division *Feldherrnhalle*, would act as a rearguard to those units falling back along the Orsha–Minsk highway by deploying on either side of it. Steinkeller met with Martinek, commander of XXXIX Panzer Corps, later that day to explain his decision.

It was during this time that Martinek was made aware that his 12th Infantry Division (*Generalleutnant* Bamler) was now the designated commander of the garrison of *Festung* Mogilev. The Commandant of Mogilev was *Generalmajor* Erdmannsdorff who, since taking up the post on 1 April 1944, had become infamous for his ruthless behaviour towards the local population.

Elsewhere, as Bamler's forces moved to take up their positions, the Soviet attacks of 26 June were turning rapidly into more of a pursuit as the German rearguard desperately tried to buy time for those formations heading to the safety of the Drut River west of Mogilev. The flank and rearguards were often composed of a nucleus of front-line infantry bolstered by less experienced formations such as security troops, who were expected to have experience of the forests and swamps from their time fighting the partisans. Unfortunately, the security units were not only poorly armed but proved to be of little value against veteran Soviet infantry, armour and artillery. One such assemblage, the 321st Division Group, which seems to have consisted of a replacement battalion, security troops and rear-echelon soldiers, was tasked with screening 110th Infantry Division's left flank.

An extract from a 110th Division memoir for 26 June puts the situation it found itself in thus: 'The Russians began to pursue - energetically. Thanks to their good motorisation and extensive armoured forces they were able, more often than not, to outflank and press the division … especially heavy fighting broke out along the Orsha–Mogilev road … the Russians succeeded in advancing up to the Dnepr, where they blocked the road with stout log barricades and mines. An attack from the south by assault guns under the command of *Generalleutnant* Schunemann [commanding 337th Infantry Division] … stalled in front of this Soviet barricade. All the while the Russians were pouring in a continuous stream of troops reaching the Dnepr and sending groups of their motorised units across the river before the German troops could reach the western bank … our divisional commander [*Generalleutnant* Kurowski] recognised the dangerous situation. He shortened our bridgehead on the eastern bank … took the 254th Infantry Regiment and sent it across to the west bank by vehicle with the assignment of establishing a southward-facing front and preventing an advance to the north-west by the Soviets.'

On the southern flank of Fourth Army, where it connected with Ninth Army, XII AC's 57th Infantry Division held the line. To its left was 267th Infantry Division and to its right were elements of 707th Security Division. From the beginning of Operation Bagration, XII AC had enjoyed a relatively quiet time despite activity on either side. The 57th Infantry Division's main defensive position lay on the western bank of the Dnepr River. However, to its rear was heavily waterlogged swampland and, 'forest (infested with) strong partisan groups'. Such was the difficulty of the ground that, 'Supply was only possible from the north, from Mogilev.' During 25 June, 'A penetration on the right wing … was cleared up, then … in the late afternoon the division's large train (transport etc.) and all other non-essential elements were evacuated to the west as a precaution. 'The following day was recorded as, 'A quiet day for the division.'

Returning to Fourth Army's left flank, 78th Assault Division, under Traut's command, had abandoned Orsha as indefensible and was now moving to join up with the remainder of XXVII AC at Dubrovka, some 30km south of Orsha. A 78th Division memoir records that, 'heavy fighting had taken place before (26 June) where the divisions few remaining assault guns had knocked out fifteen Russian tanks. During the course of 27 June, 78th, 25th Panzer Grenadier and 260th Infantry divisions had arrived. Some elements of these units had had to fight their through to the assembly area. This was the first indication of the so-called Wandering Pocket in which these three divisions were to fight their way south-west in the direction of Minsk ... The C.O. described the situation and went on to explain that it was only a matter of hours before they were encircled and that the route they were following, over poor roads and its direction dictated by the enemy, offered no likelihood of the supply of ammunition, food or fuel.'

The narrative continues with emphasis being placed on speed and mobility at the expense of, 'Everything which might hinder movement ... to be left behind. That the wounded had to suffer as a result of these measures was the (bitterest) part of all. All that mattered now was to get as many men as possible to the safety of the German lines, who knew how many kilometres to the west.'

The corps' retreat began on 28 June, the same day as some Tiger Is of Heavy Tank Battalion 501 attached themselves to this Wandering Pocket. Similar Wandering Pockets would soon be formed across the rear of AGC. Heavy Tank Battalion 501 had been involved in the fighting around Orsha from 23 June but had been committed in small groups for defensive work where required. Consequently, it was no longer a cohesive unit. However, such a small unit was nevertheless a powerful addition to the Pocket's armoured strength.

As Fourth Army's retreat towards the Dnepr and generally westwards was becoming less efficient than ordered, Zakharov, during the night of 27 June, entrusted two rifle divisions (290th and 369th) from Forty-Ninth Army and two (238th and 139th) from Fiftieth Army, to take Mogilev. Earlier that day a ring had been thrown around the city by Forty-Ninth Army's 23rd Guards Tank Brigade supported by some SU-76 self-propelled guns.

The remainder of Forty-Ninth Army was to press on to the west. By midnight on 27 June Mogilev was under attack from all directions and street fighting raged in the outlying districts throughout the early morning of 28 June. It was for behaviour during this time that *Generalmajor* Erdmannsdorff was later accused of using civilians as human shields. As the fighting drew nearer to the town centre, the Soviets offered the garrison the opportunity to surrender but it was rejected, apparently by Erdmannsdorff. At about this time several of Bamler's regimental commanders approached him with the suggestion that, as defeat was now inevitable and their men had unquestionably made an effort to carry out the Führer's orders, they should attempt a breakout. Bamler refused to countenance the idea. However, it was decided by the regimental commands to break out on their own responsibility. The divisional artillery had all been lost on the way to Mogilev, so they were unencumbered by too much heavy weaponry or similar baggage. However, the wounded would have to be left to the mercy of the Red Army. Without Bamler's blessing, units of his division now began to break off combat and break out independently. At 1800hrs on 28 June the Mogilev garrison surrendered. When Bamler was interrogated the Soviets recorded his comments as follows. 'The captured commander of the 12th Infantry Division stated: "The Mogilev garrison received an order from Hitler to hold the city at any cost. The rapid and stormy pace of the Russian offensive upset all our plans and calculations. He stunned us. We suffered heavy losses. Of the 8,000 soldiers, no more than 3,000 remained in the division. The Russians got huge trophies, including the material of the 12th Artillery Regiment.'" Although Bamler was alleged to have, 'tacitly tolerated [Erdmannsdorff's use of human shields and the execution of forced civilian labour building defences] this approach' he was tried but exonerated of this. Erdmannsdorff himself was tried in 1946 at Minsk and hanged for these and other war crimes.

Elsewhere on 28 June, as some of 12th Infantry Division's men fought their way west, Second Belarusian Front's three armies advanced a further 25km.

How the German Volunteer Worker scheme was advertised. At first the occupation authorities called for volunteers for German factories and farms but when news filtered back to their homes about conditions, volunteering collapsed. Thereafter such workers were conscripted. The numbers removed from Belarus are in the region of 400,000, some 5 per cent of the population in 1939. Their treatment post-liberation was that of traitors. (*Nik Cornish at www.stavka.photos*)

A Soviet 45mm M-42 anti-tank gun with its crew in heavily wooded terrain near Mogilev. Effective against both light German armour and infantry targets, this useful weapon was often deployed to knock out German positions as it was lightweight and manoeuvrable. (*Courtesy of the Central Museum of the Armed Forces, Moscow via Stavka*)

A SdKfz. 11/1 towing a covered 15cm *Nebelwerfer* 41 into position. The five-man crew are mounted on the vehicle. Nicknamed 'Moaning Minnie', it was a useful weapon with a range of almost 7km. However, as the missiles left a highly visible exhaust trail, it was easily spotted. As its crew had to take cover, it took some time to limber up and move and was thus vulnerable to counter-battery fire. (*Nik Cornish at www.stavka.photos*)

The early hours of 23 June were unseasonably wet. Consequently, many of the Soviet infantry went into action wearing their greatcoats. These men edge forwards covered by a sub-machine gunner. *(Courtesy of the Central Museum of the Armed Forces, Moscow via Stavka)*

Red Army intelligence noted that the German defences before Mogilev were, 'thickly protected with wire obstacles and minefields'. Soviet Sappers were equipped with heavy-duty pincers to cut, 'additional passages' through, such as that seen here. Needless to say, such obstacles as these could provide a hindrance to counter-attacks. (*Nik Cornish at www.stavka.photos*)

Waiting for one of the Luftwaffe missions flown against Second Belarusian Front's offensive, a Soviet anti-aircraft gun crew watches the skies. The Soviet history wrote, 'German air activity … revived somewhat on this day … Overall, sixty enemy air sorties were registered on this day of battle [24 June].' The gun's official designation is 37mm automatic air defence gun M1939 (61-K). *(From the fonds of the RGAKFD in Krasnogorsk via Stavka)*

On the night of 22–23 June AGC's air support, Luftflotte 6, had sent four squadrons of Heinkel He 111s to bomb Poltava airfield in Ukraine. The destruction of forty-three B-17 bombers (USAF machines refuelling after a mission over Germany) and the damaging of a further twenty-nine US aircraft, as well as destroying twenty-one Soviet fighters, was considered a victory. However, the amount of aviation fuel consumed was to drastically curtail Luftflotte 6's ability to fly ground support missions during the early days of Operation Bagration. (*Nik Cornish at www.stavka.photos*)

German artillery support and counter-battery fire was considerably less effective during late June than it had been earlier in the year due to the Soviet gunners' considerably improved practice and greater numbers of guns. This German 105mm leFH 18M's crew have their mosquito nets wrapped around their helmets as mosquitos were an ever-present irritant in the marshy ground that was prevalent before Mogilev. (*Nik Cornish at www.stavka.photos*)

As the smoke clears from the Soviet bombardment, infantrymen of XXCI Rifle Corps head for the Pronya River. They are clutching the remains of riverside fences or cottages, anything that will help them cross the river. In the background men can be seen who are already in the water. The difference in riverbank heights is apparent. (*Courtesy of the Central Museum of the Armed Forces, Moscow via Stavka*)

An unidentified security detachment prepares for a partisan sweep. When called upon to supplement the combat formations proper they were often found to be less than ready for front-line combat situations. As the situation deteriorated, those with horses were at a distinct advantage when the retreat turned into a rout and it was every man for himself. (*Nik Cornish at www.stavka.photos*)

As Second Belarusian Front reached each of the rivers before Mogilev the poor infrastructure began to take its toll. The heavy vehicles, such as tanks and fully laden lorries, churned up the approaches to the pontoon bridges often so badly that they were unusable. This in turn caused massive traffic jams that led to units falling behind. Consequently, the forward mobile groups did not get the artillery or armoured support they needed to make solid gains. For the riflemen, crossing was simpler. (*From the fonds of the RGAKFD in Krasnogorsk via Stavka*)

The Red Army did not always prove successful. Here a group of German infantry examine a knocked out T-34/76. (*Nik Cornish at www.stavka.photos*)

During the fighting around Orsha Tiger Is of Heavy Tank Battalion 501 were withdrawing when a bridge collapsed, causing the loss of one of their number. The tank had to be blown up where it lay. Several others were immobilised due to lack of fuel. The weight of these vehicles was fifty-three tons, which made them almost impossible to recover from wet ground in combat conditions. (*Nik Cornish at www.stavka.photos*)

Armoured losses were inevitable but replacements were virtually unobtainable. When the surviving armoured crews were surplus to specialist requirements they were given a gun and told to join the infantry. This panzer soldier, centre, looks somewhat bemused by his new role. *(Nik Cornish at www.stavka.photos)*

An SU-76 self-propelled gun drives into Mogilev on 28 June. Few were committed to the street fighting but they were useful in winkling out those diehards who refused to surrender by direct fire. The disadvantage for the crew was the open-topped fighting compartment, which offered no protection from grenades or fire from above. (*From the fonds of the RGAKFD in Krasnogorsk via Stavka*)

After Mogilev had been liberated the work of the engineers began. The clearance of mines, booby traps and unexploded ordnance took priority. These men do not appear to be using mine detectors. (*Courtesy of the Central Museum of the Armed Forces, Moscow via Stavka*)

Soviet riflemen, armed with PPSh-41 sub-machine guns, provide cover for advancing comrades. The PPSh-41 was an excellent weapon for such close combat situations with its high rate of fire, compact size and simplicity of maintenance. Some six million were produced by 1945. (*Nik Cornish at www.stavka.photos*)

Keeping the artillery moving forwards was a priority for all Soviet Fronts during Operation Bagration. The amount of camouflage makes it difficult to tell the types of gun waiting in this traffic jam. Despite the weakness of the Luftwaffe at this time, artillery was too important to risk. The nature of the road's surface is clearly visible here, and one summer shower would turn it to mud. (*Courtesy of the Central Museum of the Armed Forces, Moscow via Stavka*)

Chapter Five

Festung Bobruisk

When AGC captured Bobruisk on 28 June 1941, a senior German officer described the town as, 'a dump consisting mainly of wooden buildings' with an, 'extremely primitive surrounding area'. However, it was not its architectural merits or lack of them that made it a significant location, it straddled the Moscow–Minsk–Warsaw highway. It was also an important railway hub and river port. Its position on the western bank of the Berezina River and its bridges thus made it a vitally important Soviet objective during June 1944.

The planning for Bagration placed the Bobruisk area squarely in the zone of General K. K. Rokossovsky's First Belarusian Front's operations. Only the right-flank formations of First Belarusian Front were to be part of this stage of Bagration: these were, from the north, where Third Army's (Lieutenant General A. V. Gorbatov) right flank linked it with Second Belarusian Front. Its left then joined up with Forty-Eighth Army (Lieutenant General P. L. Romanenko). Romanenko's left flank abutted with Sixty-Fifth Army (Lieutenant General P. I. Batov), which shared a boundary along the banks of the Berezina with Twenty-Eighth Army (Lieutenant General A. A. Lutschinski). That in turn joined the right flank of Sixty-First Army under Lieutenant General P.A. Belov. Air support was to be provided by Sixteenth Air Army.

Rokossovsky enjoyed several advantages over the other Front commanders involved. His Third Army already occupied a considerable bridgehead on the western bank of the Dnepr River between Bykhov to the north and Rogachev to the south. This position faced the junction of German Fourth and Ninth Armies. Furthermore, Third Army's right flank ran down the Drut River to its confluence with the Dnepr at Rogachev, then followed the Dnepr until it connected with Forty-Eighth Army. Forty-Eighth Army also benefitted from an inverted, triangular bridgehead that ran from the banks of the Dnepr westward to the Berezina. Consequently, First Belarusian Front's forces faced fewer waterways to negotiate than further north. However, on the downside, both Sixty-Fifth and Twenty-Eighth Armies faced significantly difficult woody, marshy terrain criss-crossed with tributaries to the Pripet River.

Rokossovsky's memoirs describe how he planned and prepared for his Front's part in Bagration: 'Planning was preceded by extensive work in the field, where I often had literally to crawl about on all fours … I decided that it would be worth dealing two strikes on different sectors of the Front's right wing: one with Third and Forty-Eighth Armies from Rogachev towards Bobruisk to the north-west: the other with Sixty-Fifth and Twenty-Eighth Armies from the lower reaches of the Berezina to the south-west.'

This splitting of forces into two separate main offensives was contrary to Stavka's view that there should only be one main attack per Front. Rokossovsky argued that in his area this dissipation of force was vital to the achievement of success as the terrain would otherwise negate it. 'After studying the terrain and enemy defences,' he concluded, due to the size of the bridgehead that, 'we could assemble only the Third and part of the Forty-Eighth Armies in the Rogachev area,' but, 'If this group were not assisted by a strike on another sector the enemy might well prevent a breakthrough, as he would have ample opportunity to bring up forces from [unthreatened] sectors. Two main attacks dealt with the situation more effectively.'

When Rokossovsky put his plan to Stalin and Stavka he added, 'success achieved on only one of these sectors would place the enemy forces in a difficult situation, the enemy would be denied any real possibility of manoeuvre and enable our Front to step up the offensive'. Despite senior officers' objections, Stalin granted Rokossovsky permission to carry out his plan.

Happily, Third Army's bridgehead was suitable for action by all arms, while that in Forty-Eighth Army's zone to the south was more problematic. As Rokossovsky described it, it was 'one huge marsh dotted with small islands of scrub and dense forest. There were no conditions for concentrating tanks and heavy artillery, a road even for a light gun would require several layers of logs. I therefore ordered Lieutenant General P. L. Romanenko to regroup his main forces on the Rogachev bridgehead on the left flank of Third Army and act jointly with (it): the units (of Forty-Eighth Army) remaining in the Berezina Bridgehead were to pin down as many enemy forces as possible and thereby facilitate the main attack.'

Rokossovsky was fulsome in his praise of partisan operations but it is a quote from a post-war German report with reference to the partisans' activities that makes the point well. 'Realising German resistance would be strongest on both sides of the (ruined) bridge site, the Russians decided to establish a bridgehead at the most unlikely point – in the worst swamps possible … they established a foothold on two small islands.' The Germans ignored this, thinking the area too swampy. 'It turned out to be a serious mistake.' During the course of the next few nights, 'the Russians began to build an underwater bridge … about two metres wide … consisting of previously assembled trestles … with the planking about four inches below the surface. This presented no technical difficulties because of the very slow current of the Pripet River. Its existence was not suspected until a few Russian anti-tank guns suddenly appeared on the north [German-held] bank of the river'.

German efforts to destroy the bridge failed but a Soviet attack managed to increase the area of the bridgeheads. Further German counter-attacks failed to dislodge the Soviet troops. As the report finally noted, 'The Russians consolidated the bridgehead during the following days and then used it as one of the jump-off bases for their large-scale summer offensives.'

With his preparations complete and Moscow's approval, it was up to Rokossovsky to carry through the operations that would link the men of his Front with those of Third Belarusian Front with the closure of their pincers west of Minsk.

Standing in First Belarusian Front's way was Ninth Army. This had been commanded by *General der Infanterie* Hans Jordan since 20 May 1944, prior to which he led VI AC. His new command, running from north to south, consisted of XXXV AC, which connected with Fourth Army's XII AC, XLI Panzer Corps (no tanks), and LV AC, which formed the link with Second Army's XXIII AC. Although Ninth Army's only embedded armour consisted of seventy-six StuG III assault guns, it did have the possibility of support from AGC's reserve 20th Panzer Division stationed near Bobruisk. The disposition of the StuG III units was interesting. The bulk of these, some fifty-nine vehicles, were divided between the five infantry divisions of XXXV AC facing Soviet Third Army's bridgehead at the Drut–Dnepr confluence. The remaining seventeen StuG IIIs, in XLI Panzer Corp's infantry divisions, faced the Forty-Eighth Army's bridgehead from the Dnepr to the Berezina rivers. LV AC had not one StuG III to help repel any attacks on its front, where the Pripet Marshes and waterways were expected to prevent the deployment of armour by the Soviets. Following the German line westwards from the junction of Ninth and Second Armies, the latter having on 22 June seventy-five StuG IIIs, there was also a paucity of armour for much the same reason. AGC's HQ was clearly hoping for a wet summer.

In common with the other Front's opening moves, First Belarusian Front's armies launched the usual reconnaissance attacks during the night of 23 June. These were all beaten back but then everything changed for the Germans of XXXV AC on Ninth Army's right wing. Marshall Zhukov, co-ordinating First and Second Belarusian fronts, had left Rokossovsky joking that he and Gorbatov would, 'reach out over the Berezina and pull us out of the marshes to Bobruisk'. Rokossovsky had attached himself to Twenty-Eighth Army to monitor its progress to the south. When the bombardment of XXXV AC ended at 0430hrs, shelling had been switched, roughly halfway through, from the front lines to the rear areas as Sixteenth Air Army unleashed a rolling stream of ground-attack missions on the forward positions. The dazed and deafened German infantry emerged from the ruins of their trenches and bunkers to witness waves of Soviet riflemen, screaming their battle cry, a long, drawn-out 'Urrrah', as they crossed the swampy ground and parts of the Drut River over underwater bridges, following tanks heading for them along what had to be corduroy roads.

Despite the 'shock and awe' created by the Soviet bombardments and ground-attacks, as Rokossovsky put it, 'During the first day the Third Army achieved little success … and (was) then forced to dig in. The offensive on Forty-Eighth Army's sector also ran into difficulties. The wide marshy plain of the Drut River impeded the infantry but especially the armour. It took two hours to knock the Nazis out of the front-line trenches, and the second line was not captured until noon.' However, when the breakthrough came it was made at the junction between 134th and 296th Infantry Divisions, precisely where Ninth and Fourth Armies connected. These units had a mere four StuG IIIs, subordinate to the former, which claimed to have accounted for thirty Soviet tanks. But this was not the only worrying development for Ninth Army; on XLI Panzer Corps' front things were going rather worse for Jordan's forces. The Soviet bombardment had started some twenty minutes later than that to the north and, during the course of the morning, a major breakthrough in 36th Infantry Division's lines had been made by XVIII Rifle Corps. With significant air support, five lines of defence had been penetrated to a depth of 5 to

6km. To quote Rokossovsky, 'This enabled General Batov [Sixty-Fifth Army] to throw ... I Guards Tank Corps into the breach, and it swiftly moved into the rear of the Germans ...' However, Twenty-Eighth Army had made little progress by day's end.

Rokossovsky summed up progress in the southern sector thus, 'The southern strike group broke through the enemy defences on a 30km front to a depth of five to ten kilometres ... the tanks extended this breakthrough to a depth of 20km.' He commented on the northern sector, saying, '... fighting continued all night on 24 June. The enemy counter-attacked repeatedly, striving to knock the wedge we had driven back into the river. This ... he was unable to do.'

Zhukov telephoned Rokossovsky, congratulating him on the successes of the day and saying, 'it was we who would now have to reach out to Gorbatov from the southern bank of the Berezina'. Doubtless Rokossovsky informed Zhukov that he was planning to exploit the favourable situation in the south by committing his Front's Cavalry-Mechanised Group on 25 June between Sixty-Fifth and Twenty-Eighth Armies.

However, Jordan had not been idle. Busch had granted him permission to deploy 20th Panzer Division in support of XXXV AC, north-east of Bobruisk. That evening the 20th Panzer Division's Panzer IVs engaged with Soviet armour and achieved some success in stabilising the position. Unfortunately for Ninth Army, the breakthrough to the south of Bobruisk in 36th Infantry Division's sector seemed to pose a greater threat. Possibly Jordan was overly optimistic about XXXV AC's ability to hold the line north of Bobruisk and therefore ordered 20th Panzer Division to disengage from combat, drive 100km, over narrow dirt roads and restore the hole in XLI Panzer Corps' defences. However, by the time the 20th Panzer Division arrived it was too late to restore the situation as the breach had grown to some 40km, which, despite claiming sixty Soviet tanks, the Germans were unable to fill.

While desperately attempting to shore up Ninth Army's southern flank Jordan's forces north-east of Bobruisk were also now in danger of collapse as its five division-strong XXXV AC was pushed back as its fifty-nine StuG IIIs were unable to stem the Soviet tide. The only other reserve unit, 707th Security Division, committed to restoring the link with Fourth Army, had failed in its efforts having been brushed aside as the roads to Bobruisk, to the rear of XXXV AC, came under threat.

On 25 June Jordan requested permission from Busch to pull his main forces, particularly XXXV AC, back to the west and north. Unsurprisingly, AGC's commander refused. In Ninth Army's War Diary it was noted, 'Having made a responsible report, one must accept the orders of his superiors even when he is convinced of the opposite. What is worse is to know that the completely inadequate directive from the Army Group is not the product of purposeful leadership trying to do its utmost but merely an attempt to carry out orders long overtaken by events.'

During the early hours of the same day, Soviet aerial reconnaissance, untroubled by any Luftwaffe interference, reported, 'the movement of large enemy columns of artillery, motor vehicles, and horse drawn transport, which was spread out along the roads to the west, toward Bobruisk'. When he received this information, Gorbatov, commanding Third Army, immediately ordered the entirety of IX Tank Corps to occupy a position some

15km north of Bobruisk to cut off the retreat of German forces along the paved road to Mogilev, thus forcing them to use poorer roads heading towards Bobruisk.

Nor was Ninth Army's situation any better. XLI Panzer Corps too fell back, east of the Berezina River from south to north, where it hoped to reach the bridges leading into Bobruisk. In an attempt to secure these bridges, 20th Panzer Division was sent ahead but advancing Soviet forces were already heading in the same direction. Their swift arrival prevented the panzers from securing positions around any ground further north than the railway bridge into the city, which was difficult to approach other than along the exposed, steeply banked railway line. Following in the panzers' wake was a huge convoy of mixed transport, ambulances, trucks and the inevitable, innumerable horse-drawn wagons: very rapidly an immense traffic jam developed as units jostled for priority crossing rights. The 'poor bloody infantry' counted themselves lucky as they could at least make their own way across to the apparent safety of Bobruisk on foot.

That afternoon Ninth Army, recognising that its situation was worsening minute by minute, transferred command of its as yet unengaged LV AC to Second Army and also moved its HQ to Maryina Gorka, less than 40km south-east of Minsk. Here it would link up with 12th Panzer Division, supported by the weak and inexperienced 390th Field Training Infantry Division that was transferring from AGN via Minsk to establish a line in that area and hold open a route westward for Ninth Army. Ironically, 12th Panzer Division had been a part of AGC, in the Bobruisk area, until placed in reserve to the rear of AGN for refitting and re-equipping. Nevertheless, it was missing its flak and reconnaissance units and its armour was understrength, counting only forty-four Panzer IIIs and IVs.

With elements of two army corps stuck in and around the area of Bobruisk, the city was close to being surrounded as the Soviets had taken possession of the bridges, 15km north of the city centre, at no cost as they had been left undefended. Unable to move easily into Bobruisk, XXXV AC's combat units fought desperately to allow some of the rear-echelon formations to reach safety. Along with XLI Panzer Corps' troops, there were roughly 75,000 men now cut off. Those that could, having abandoned their weapons and vehicles, crossed the railway bridge to reach the eastern bank of the Berezina. Even this vague sanctuary was better than leaving friendly positions for an escape route in the forests and swamps, where they could be shot out of hand by the Red Army or suffer a worse fate at the hands of a vengeful group of civilians or partisans.

The Commandant of Bobruisk was the recently appointed (20 June 1944) commander of 383rd Infantry Division (the city's allocated garrison), *Generalmajor* Hamann. Very little of significance had been done to prepare the city for defence, although some strongpoints and trenches had been constructed. On 27 June Hamann received the order that Bobruisk was to be held to the last man and to the last round under all circumstances. Busch's latest reply to Jordan's most recent request to allow a breakout was in much the same vein. However, on 27 June Jordan was relieved of his command, to be replaced by *General der Panzertruppe* Nikolaus von Vormann, due to Jordan's mishandling of 20th Panzer Division's counter-attacks.

The first major series of Soviet attacks mounted in an attempt to capture the city off the march failed. Indeed, Sixteenth Air Army's bombing provided very useful rubble for the Germans to improvise defences and would prove a handicap for armoured vehicles supporting infantry attacks. Luckily for the Germans, the night of 27–28 June was relatively quiet and enabled more men of both XXXV and XLI Panzer Corps to make their way into the city. Rokossovsky assigned CV Rifle Corps of Sixty-Fifth Army to liberate Bobruisk, with the attack to begin in the early hours of 28 June. As the first Soviet troops stormed forward shouting 'Urrah', they were met by a wall of fire from their desperate opponents. Nevertheless, progress was steady as house by house and street by street by street the Landser, ordinary German soldiers, fell back. At 0825hrs *Generalleutnant* Hoffmeister, commanding XLI Panzer Corps, radioed Ninth Army HQ from inside Bobruisk as follows: '383rd Infantry Division is engaged in fighting for Bobruisk. In the city are the commanders of 36th and 45th Infantry Divisions and 707th Security Division. Commander of 134th Infantry Division has shot himself. Since dark elements of every division have been streaming into Bobruisk in disorder … flow across the railway bridge continues. No radio contact with XXXV AC, which ordered all guns blown up. Request complete freedom of action.'

AGC's reply came over four hour later stating, 'On orders of the Führer, Feste Platz Bobruisk is to be abandoned, surrounded units are to break out toward the north along the Berezina'. Ninth Army's War Diary recorded, 'This morning's report of the catastrophe involving the main body of Ninth Army surrounded in the area around Bobruisk leaves no doubt that the unit has no more fighting value, even if the intended breakout battles could be successfully carried out.'

As fighting raged in and around Bobruisk, German staff officers frantically tried to organise the breakout that was timed to start at 2300hrs from the northern and north-western districts of the city. Rumour and counter-rumour spread like wildfire among the disorganised mass of men and Belarusian civilians who made their way to the assembly areas, desperate to escape the Red Army. The 20th Panzer Division's remaining tanks and any available assault guns would provide the spearhead. According to Soviet sources, the armour involved numbered 'forty-two tanks and self-propelled guns'. Remarkably, considering the continual fighting, the attempt was only thirty minutes late in beginning.

Rokossovsky remembered in his memoirs, 'Officers and men, all of them drunk, attacked in wave after wave in spite of the deadly fire of our artillery … at the cost of great losses the Nazis succeeded in driving several wedges into the defences.' According to other sources, German troops burst out singing, 'O Germany in honour', or chanted, 'We want to go home'. Incredibly, this first breakout succeeded as the Soviet line at this point was wafer thin due to the redeployment of I Guard Tank Corps. However, as Sixty-Fifth Army's staff recovered from its initial shock, the long, straggling German column came under increasing fire as CV Rifle Corps redeployed units and, as dawn broke, the Soviet air attacks began. Rapidly, the column began to lose shape, breaking down into ad hoc *Kampfgruppen* (battle groups) led by junior officers or NCOs. Many of these headed off-road to avoid the tanks and aircraft, which seemed to be ubiquitous. Despite the chaos behind it, the vanguard had, by mid-morning, advanced some 35km to the north-west.

Meanwhile, in Bobruisk two further breakouts were attempted during the morning of 29 June. One was encircled and virtually destroyed, having made a mere 5km, and the final effort by the rearguard was overrun before it even began. Some 5,000 wounded were not included in these efforts and remained behind. A veteran of the 134th Infantry Division recalled, 'So we were surrounded and those who were at the front shouted, "Advance guns and anti-aircraft guns!" ... and the ones from behind: "We're out of ammunition." ... and so it went on forever ... it was all shit.'

Another survivor, from 6th Infantry Division, noted, 'On the 29 June the Russians occupied the hospital ... about an hour later, Russians appeared in oil-smeared uniforms. They systematically went from bed to bed pointing their sub-machine guns and emptying their magazines ... I lay in this hospital for three more days ... suddenly a Russian civilian doctor appeared ... the doctor ensured that the survivors were driven out of the room [to a former Wehrmacht rest home].'

Hamann himself was taken prisoner on 28 or 29 June and, among his other crimes, his regime was accused of using the blood of Belarusian children to treat German wounded. The children were then killed. The mass grave of these unfortunates was discovered when a survivor led Red Army men to the burial site. Hamann was tried for war crimes and hanged in Bryansk in December 1945.

As the remnants of the garrison and those who had not escaped the Soviet net were rounded up, the official date of Bobruisk's liberation was being transmitted throughout the USSR as Thursday, 29 June. Rokossovsky wrote that both Sixty-Fifth and Forty-Eighth Armies were responsible for this accomplishment. The latter was included because, with the support of the Danube River Flotilla, it had crossed the Berezina River almost at the last minute before the surrender.

For the Germans in the new 'Wandering Pockets' of Ninth Army, all there was to celebrate was judged by how they survived, day by day, on the march back to their own lines.

A Luftwaffe ground crew prepares an He 177 for a mission on 25 June by Combat Squadron 1 (*Kampfgeschwader*) *Hindenburg* to bomb the HQ of First Belarusian Front's XXC Rifle Corps. The following day this heavy bomber unit attacked the important railway hubs at Kalinkavichy, Gomel and Velikiye Luki. An attack on 2nd Guards Tank Army's advancing forces, undertaken on 28 July, was this unit's final operation before lack of aviation fuel and heavy losses – 25 per cent of its aircraft were lost – led to it being removed from the Eastern Front and disbanded. (*Nik Cornish at www.stavka.photos*)

The proximity of 20th Panzer Division to Bobruisk was certainly to Ninth Army's advantage in June 1944. It was a strong unit, fielding fifty-six Panzer IVs, such as this one having its track repaired. It also included seven Panzer IIIs. *Generalmajor* Mortimer von Kessel, its commander, had been with the division for more than a year when Operation Bagration began. (*Nik Cornish at www.stavka.photos*)

Facing Ninth Army, First Belarusian Front could deploy some 1,300 tanks and AFVs, including seventy-two engineer tanks such as flamethrower and mine-clearance vehicles. These T34/85s are ticking over on one of the better-quality roads in the region. Their broad tracks were of more use on wet ground than the narrow ones of the Panzer IVs and StuG IIIs opposing them. *(Courtesy of the Central Museum of the Armed Forces, Moscow via Stavka)*

Three NKL-27 skiffs of the Dnepr Military Flotilla operating on the Berezina River. With a two-man crew, these plywood vessels were used for a variety of tasks such as patrolling, supply movements and transporting up to ten riflemen. They were generally attached to pontoon bridging units, which were essential formations during Operation Bagration due to the number of waterways. (*Courtesy of the Central Museum of the Armed Forces, Moscow via Stavka*)

Facing the Dnepr River Flotilla were a handful of such extemporised *Kanonenboot* (gunboat). *Breslau*, seen here, is one such. The crew appear to be soldiers and the vessel is armed with a former Soviet 76mm M1902/30, which retains its wheels. The original caption states only that it is deployed on the Pripet River and is dated 20 June 1944. (*Nik Cornish at www.stavka.photos*)

As Rokossovsky noted, 'We gave the partisans specific tasks concerning where and when to strike at Nazi communications and bases. They blew up trains on the Bobruisk–Minsk … and other railways … [all partisan operations] were subordinated to the purposes of the forthcoming operation.' (*Courtesy of the Central Museum of the Armed Forces, Moscow via Stavka*)

The Red Army had, by mid-1944, reduced its use of armoured trains, such as this BP-43 type, due to the speed of its advance being so much faster than the time it took to repair and re-gauge the tracks destroyed by the Germans. It is interesting to note that when Rokossovsky visited the HQ of his forces not engaged in the early part of Operation Bagration, they were quartered in an armoured train due to the activities of Ukrainian Nationalist partisans in the area. Not all partisans were Soviet sympathisers. (*Courtesy of the Central Museum of the Armed Forces, Moscow via Stavka*)

When conditions were difficult the Germans built artificial islands of solid ground to act as supporting bases for their three -or four-man lookout posts dotted throughout the marshy riverbank of the Pripet River. These were designed to act as early warning points rather than substantial defences. (*Nik Cornish at www.stavka.photos*)

At 0430hrs on 24 June Soviet Third Army's artillery opened up with every available gun, mortar and rocket within range of XXXV AC's positions. The guns shown here are 122mm M-30 howitzers, capable of firing 5–6 rounds per minute. It also had good anti-tank capabilities. *(Courtesy of the Central Museum of the Armed Forces, Moscow via Stavka)*

With much of its front-line defences destroyed by artillery and aerial bombardment, XXXV AC's infantry took position where they could. This MG 34 team at least has a good, clear field of fire. *(Nik Cornish at www.stavka.photos)*

The German infantry viewed such suddenly, but murkily, populated Soviet crossing points as this with utter disbelief. The shadowy figures of lightly equipped Soviet riflemen are clutching guidelines to keep them on the right path and moving as quickly as they can before the smoke disperses and the Germans can see their targets clearly. The Soviet attack began at 0600hrs Moscow Time. (*Courtesy of the Central Museum of the Armed Forces, Moscow via Stavka*)

Even worse than enemy infantry were the tanks that followed them. Here a T-34/85 moves on to the bank, having crossed by yet another concealed bridge. (*Courtesy of the Central Museum of the Armed Forces, Moscow via Stavka*)

The Soviet General Staff Study of late 1944 records, 'While destroying the enemy's personnel and equipment … (our) tanks ran into the enemy's solid columns of artillery, supply trains and motor transport. They broke into the columns at high speed, firing on the move. The enemy's burning tanks, abandoned motor vehicles and piles of destroyed transport more and more often forced IX Tank Corps to halt.' Here several Red Army troops consider the German wreckage. (*From the fonds of the RGAKFD in Krasnogorsk via Stavka*)

With so much artillery abandoned, the Landser's only hope to hold off enemy armour was the trusty *Panzerfaust*, such as the type 60 shown here. By the late war experience had taught Soviet tacticians to attach infantry platoons to heavy armoured companies to protect against Panzerfaust-armed tank hunter units in urban areas. (*Nik Cornish at www.stavka.photos*)

The German troops crammed into the Bobruisk Cauldron presented a wonderful target for such unsubtle weapons as these Katyusha rocket launchers. Designed more for saturation bombardment than accuracy, the Katyusha was also a weapon whose noise alone instilled terror into those who waited below for its projectiles to strike. (*From the fonds of the RGAKFD in Krasnogorsk via Stavka*)

With minimal air cover, XLI Panzer Corps' position at the Berezina railway bridge was reliant on its own anti-aircraft assets for protection against the conveyor belt-like Soviet air attacks. This quadruple-barrelled 20mm weapon is typical of the weapons employed, as long as they could be found suitable positions in the chaotic traffic at the bridgehead. (*Nik Cornish at www.stavka.photos*)

A Soviet mortar team changes position during the street fighting for Bobruisk. The Red Army was a prolific user of mortars for close infantry support. (*Courtesy of the Central Museum of the Armed Forces, Moscow via Stavka*)

The remnants of a German strongpoint in Bobruisk. The original caption reads, 'A Fascist anti-tank post that failed to fulfil its task, a victim of its arch foe.' (*Courtesy of the Central Museum of the Armed Forces, Moscow via Stavka*)

The Germans deployed a number of armoured trains in the rear of AGC to support operations against partisan units. This BP-42 and another earlier model were destroyed by their crews in Bobruisk on 27 June. (*Courtesy of the Central Museum of the Armed Forces, Moscow via Stavka*)

A pair of 88mm anti-aircraft guns, with their breeches blown out, in a Soviet dump. Bobruisk had been the base for the Luftwaffe's 18th Flak Division. All its guns were lost and few of the men escaped to German lines. Involved in the retreat from Bobruisk, the 88s provided a powerful source of anti-tank defence until their ammunition ran out. (*Courtesy of the Central Museum of the Armed Forces, Moscow via Stavka*)

Chapter Six

The Polotsk Operation and Elsewhere

With the liberation of Bobruisk, AGC's front line of *Feste Platz* had been shattered within a week, and three out of its four armies were severely depleted and falling back towards the presumed safety of the Berezina River. Many junior officers and other ranks were convinced that defensive works had been built there in the months before Bagration and that it would provide some respite from the Soviet onslaught; however, this was not the case, as the more senior officers were aware.

With its left flank now exposed as Ninth Army pulled back but with its right flank still firmly connected to AGNU's First Hungarian Army west of Kovel, Weiß's Second Army remained untroubled, lined up along and behind the Pripet River and marshes. Second Army's position was an area of significant partisan activity, which was reflected in its four army corps' order of battle and dispositions. XXIII AC on the far left joined with Ninth Army's right flank and included 7th Infantry and 203rd Security Divisions as well as 17th Panzergrenadier Brigade, which was a weak regiment of training and replacement troops. On its right was XX AC's Corps Abteilung E, which had been cobbled together earlier in the year from the remnants of three infantry divisions and 3rd Cavalry Brigade. Finally, connecting AGC with AGNU, lay VIII AC with 211th Infantry, 5th Jager and 12th Hungarian Infantry Divisions. All these units were lightly armed and thinly spread along the army's nearly 300km long front.

As the marshes were so widespread and dense, a Soviet attack was deemed virtually impossible and it was believed that the real threat was posed by partisan activity, particularly the disruption of road and rail communications. In reserve, Weiß held the 4th Cavalry Brigade and two further Hungarian infantry divisions. Armoured support consisted of seventy or so StuG III assault guns distributed between the cavalry and infantry units. Facing them was the balance of First Belarusian Front: one tank and four infantry armies. When Rokossovsky's forces struck at Ninth Army, Second Army was left almost untroubled. There was a weak attack on 3rd Cavalry Brigade that was easily repelled but this was not a serious effort, merely a part of the Red Army's plan to confuse the deployment of AGC's reserves.

XL and XLI Rifle Corps were finishing off the enemy encircled around Bobruisk, (its) main forces were pursuing the remains of the defeated German-Fascist forces along the Bobruisk–Minsk and Bobruisk–Slutsk axis. Besides this, Sixty-First Army (supported by the Dnepr River Flotilla) had begun a local offensive along the Pinsk operational axes against Second Army.' As Rokossovsky recorded, 'Naturally, all of this told on the speed of developing the offensive along the main Minsk axes.'

Then First Belarusian Front's situation took a turn for the better. During the course of 29–30 June, the Front regrouped and introduced fresh units from the reserve. This allowed the impetus of the advance to continue and to comply with Stavka's directive that instructed it to, 'Launch its attack on Minsk with its right flank from the south and south-east, while the Cavalry-Mechanised Group and the Sixty-Fifth and Twenty-Eighth Armies were to attack to Baranovichi.' Furthermore, First Belarusian Front was to act, 'in conjunction with first, Third Belarusian and then Second Belarusian fronts, to encircle and destroy the enemy's Minsk group of forces'. However, the result of Rokossovsky's operations had, by 30 June, increased the frontage of his right wing by over 100km and many of his units were now well over 150km, and in some cases 300km, from their main supply bases, with many facing, 'a great need for fuel and ammunition'.

Returning to the north, First Baltic Front's three armies – Forty–Third, connecting with Third Belarusian Front's right wing, Sixth Guards in the centre and Fourth Shock on the right – had only really engaged with the latter two armies during the early days of Bagration and then mainly to support Third Belarussian Front. Fourth Shock was the weakest of Bagramyan's armies and its sole achievement had been the capture of a village, Rovnoe, between Vitebsk and Polotsk, until its strength was doubled to two rifle corps on 27 June. At this point it engaged with AGN's Sixteenth Army's understrength 205th and 24th Infantry Divisions. This action had prevented the German divisions from threatening the right flank and rear of Sixth Guards Army, which had units moving directly to the west of Polotsk. Forty-Third Army was now heading westwards to the transport hub of Lepel, roughly 110km west of Vitebsk, which fell to units of First Baltic and Third Belarusian fronts on 28 June.

As First Baltic Front progressed to the west and north-west, by 28 June Stavka issued its updated orders for the next stage. Bagramyan was instructed to capture *Feste Platz* Polotsk and, 'guarantee from the north the operations of the Belarusian Fronts in defeating the enemy in the Minsk area'. Taking Polotsk would give the fronts further north, 'the opportunity to further attack along the right bank of the Western Dvina River towards Dvinsk [Daugavpils]' in Latvia. To ensure the, 'successful advance of First Baltic Front's forces to the west, Glubokoe' [on the road to Lithuania] would also be taken. Bagramyan detailed Fourth Shock and Sixth Armies to the liberation of Polotsk; the latter would receive support from I Tank Corps, which was tasked with taking Glubokoe. Fourth Shock would outflank Polotsk from the north-east, while Sixth Guards units would strike from the south and south-west. The move to the north-west by First Baltic Front effectively ended its participation in major operations against AGC.

In and around Polotsk were units from several German divisions from both Third Panzer's and AGN's Sixteenth Armies, which defended this sector of AGN's front. *Generaloberst* Lindemann, commanding AGN, had requested that Sixteenth Army be withdrawn to the north-west around Daugavpils, but to no avail. Polotsk was to be held. Lindemann tendered his resignation but this was refused and he was ordered to restore the connection with AGC by counter-attacking with a couple of divisions and some forty-four StuG IIIs. In Polotsk the commander of the garrison, *Generalleutnant* Hilpert, commanding AGN's I AC, had two infantry divisions with which to defend Polotsk. The town enjoyed good defensible terrain including small lakes, marshes and woodland, parts of which were held by various formations of Third Panzer Army.

Fourth Shock Army's attack to the north began at 0840hrs on 29 June but made no headway. However, to the south-west, Sixth Guards Army was making progress, albeit slow, plodding through lakes and marshes. By the end of the following day the Sixth Guards Army's right flank units had advanced some 18km and were approaching Polotsk itself. Therefore, Bagramyan, in the words of the Stavka study of Bagration, 'On 30 June … demanded that the Fourth Shock Army decisively pursue the retreating enemy units with its main forces … outflanking Polotsk from the north.' Fourth Shock's commander, General Malyshev, having spent three years under investigation during Stalin's purge of the armed forces in the late 1930s, took the hint and drove his men forward ruthlessly. On 1 July Fourth Shock Army's left flank, now including the 16th Lithuanian Rifle Division, pushed ahead and reached suburban Polotsk, cutting Hilpert's exit route to the north by 3 July. The Lithuanian Division was a politically titled force as fewer than 40 per cent of its men were native Lithuanians. There were similar formations of Estonians and Latvians. These divisions would be used for propaganda and recruiting purposes when they entered their homelands later that summer. Meanwhile, Sixth Guards Army's right-flank troops had, during the same period, broken into the town. However, Hilpert was not prepared to sacrifice his men as had been the case with other *Festung Platz*. Nor was Sixteenth Army's leader, Lindemann, inclined to fight to the last man. On his own authority, Lindemann had called off the feeble attempt at a counter-attack and, remarkably, was permitted to authorise the abandonment of Polotsk, which Hilpert executed in short order. By withdrawing his I AC and other troops that had straggled in from Third Panzer Army, he was able to pull back and establish a defensive position to the north. For these actions Hilpert was awarded the Oak Leaves to his Knight's Cross of the Iron Cross on 8 August and Lindemann was allowed to relinquish command of AGN on 4 July, the same day that Polotsk was officially liberated. One of Lindemann's successor's first duties was to report that, on 5 July, AGN still had not managed to restore its connection with AGC's left flank, which was now hanging in the air.

Again quoting the Stavka study noted above, 'However, we were not able to encircle and completely destroy the enemy's Polotsk group of forces. The reason for this was the insufficiently rapid outflanking movement by Fourth Shock Army from the north.' Furthermore, it commented that, 'The capture of Polotsk, in a way, opened the gates for the subsequent advance by our forces toward the Gulf of Riga' and that, 'The Front's chief objective – the isolation of AGN from AGC – was successfully accomplished.'

For some citizens of the USSR, the Red Army's march to the west was not a good thing. From the earliest days of Operation Barbarossa in 1941, ordinary captured Soviet soldiers had volunteered for service with the Wehrmacht in many capacities, from servants to soldiers to simple labourers. Those not in combat units were known to the Germans as *Hilfswilliger* (auxiliary helper), shortened to Hiwis. By the summer of 1944 there were tens of thousands of them in the Heer; usually they had volunteered simply to get decent rations or a chance of life outside the hell of a German POW camp behind the Eastern Front. Few were politically motivated, they merely wanted a chance of survival. These men and women were often left to their own devices in times of retreat, and so it was during Bagration. They were also known as Vlasovites after the Soviet General, A. A. Vlasov, who joined the Germans in 1942 and formed the collaborationist Russian Liberation Army. Vlasov was captured in Czechoslovakia by the Red Army and hanged in 1946. A Soviet veteran of Bagration recorded the following incident he witnessed: 'I saw the first Hiwis in Belarus in the summer of 1944. Our soldiers would sometimes settle accounts with them on their own initiative, right on the spot of their capture: "Aaah, compatriots, traitors, to hell with you, damned Vlasov gang, dogs!" They were lucky if they were shot or hanged immediately. It also happened that they were tortured for a long time and finally trampled to death.'

Nor were these the only prisoners taken by the Soviet troops to undergo immediate, summary justice. A Soviet partisan recalled, 'On July 4th [1944] the Soviet army came towards Myadsel [west of Polotsk]. The Wehrmacht soldiers wanted to defend Myadsel in a ring. They fought until the Red Army came, but then had to surrender. After the surrender, the soldiers of the Wehrmacht and the police had to stand in a line. The soldiers were handed over to the Red Army as prisoners of war, the police officers to the partisans. The police officers were shot.' It was into this theatre of military disaster that *Generalfeldmarschall* Walter Model now walked.

The Hungarian 1st Cavalry Division arrived to join Second Army on 21–22 June and was assigned to anti-partisan operations. However, when Ninth Army began to retire it was sent east to support Second Army's left flank. It included around seventy-five domestically built Toldi light (seen here with its 20mm gun) and heavy tanks (40mm gun). They were of little value against Soviet armour. Nevertheless, the Germans were pleased with the Hungarian performance. *(Nik Cornish at www.stavka.photos)*

German cavalry of either the Third or Fourth Brigades on patrol on drier ground in the Pripet region. Each cavalry brigade had an attached brigade of 18 StuG IIIs and these armoured fighting vehicles constituted half of Second Army's entire armoured assets which were all StuG III assault guns. (*Nik Cornish at www.stavka.photos*)

A Hungarian machine team of one of the three Hungarian infantry divisions with Second Army. These units constituted the Hungarian II Reserve Corps. They are operating a Schwarzlose m.7/31 machine gun. A simple weapon to make and maintain, it was very useful in wetlands where constant care was imperative. These formations were less well equipped than their German allies. *(Nik Cornish at www.stavka.photos)*

Soviet gunners manning a 76mm M1927 regimental gun prepare to support an attack on Second Army. This weapon was solid and reliable, and used widely in the close infantry support role. The crew's personal weapons are Mosin-Nagant M1938 carbines. (*From the fonds of the RGAKFD in Krasnogorsk via Stavka*)

Partisans assisting regular army scouts, *Razvedchiki*, searching for routes through the Pripet Marshes on Second Army's front. Trained for deep penetration missions and encouraged to use their initiative, the *Razvedchiki* were among the Red Army's elite formations. (*Courtesy of the Central Museum of the Armed Forces, Moscow via Stavka*)

A Soviet rifleman covers an advancing comrade as they move into a burning village in southern Belarus. When time permitted, the retreating Germans destroyed anything that could be of use to their enemies. (*Courtesy of the Central Museum of the Armed Forces, Moscow via Stavka*)

A survivor of Stalin's purges during the 1930s, K. K. Rokossovsky (centre) rose to become a Marshal of the Soviet Union when Bobruisk was liberated. Here, in February 1944 when still a General of the Army, he pores over maps with Colonel General M. S. Malinin, his Chief of Staff for more than three years. (*Courtesy of the Central Museum of the Armed Forces, Moscow via Stavka*)

Sitting in the front seat of his Jeep, General of the Army I. K. Bagramyan. An Armenian by birth, he was a veteran of the First World War and joined the Red Army in late 1920. He was promoted to Marshal of the Soviet Union in 1955. (*Courtesy of the Central Museum of the Armed Forces, Moscow via Stavka*)

A formation of StuG IIIs moves into position for the abortive counter-attack around Polotsk. They are parked up under tree cover and camouflaged to avoid air observation. They have been treated with Zimmerit anti-magnetic paste to protect against magnetic mines. (*Nik Cornish at www.stavka.photos*)

Whenever possible and time allowed, the German railway troops tore up the track, using a locomotive equipped with a ploughshare that when reversed lowered the ploughshare, tearing up the rail ties as seen here. (*Courtesy of the Central Museum of the Armed Forces, Moscow via Stavka*)

A Soviet machine gun team waits to go into the attack. The central machine gun is a DP 7.62 light machine gun nicknamed the 'record player' due to its disc-shaped magazine, whereas the other men have PPS-43 sub-machine guns. The PPS was very popular with front-line troops as it was less prone to jamming than other models and was a good blunt instrument in hand-to-hand combat. (*Courtesy of the Central Museum of the Armed Forces, Moscow via Stavka*)

A gun team of Sixth Guards Army prepares to fire from cover. On his right breast the spotter is wearing the Guards badge and on his left his decorations. This latter was a tradition the Red Army had continued from Tsarist days. The gun is a Model 1943 76mm Regimental gun, a valuable weapon. It was lighter than its predecessor, the M 27, with greater traverse and capable of firing an anti-tank projectile. (*Courtesy of the Central Museum of the Armed Forces, Moscow via Stavka*)

A German machine gun team, armed with an MG 34, moves up to take position in a support line near Polotsk. Although the MG 42 was in widespread use, the MG 34 was still invaluable. (*Nik Cornish at www.stavka.photos*)

An image that could be taken anywhere along AGC's front line where swamps, lakes and waterlogged ground formed much of the battlefield. (*Nik Cornish at www.stavka.photos*)

Non-uniformed members of RONA (the Russian National Liberation Army), aka the Kaminski Brigade, parade for the camera. Relocated from the Lokot region, just to the east of Belarus, this collaborationist formation and their families was resettled in and around Lepel near Vitebsk, where it took part in various anti-partisan operations during the weeks prior to the start of Operation Bagration. With a reputation for cruelty, rapine and ill discipline, the RONA was absorbed into the Waffen SS in June 1944 as part of *Kampgruppe Gottberg*. (*Nik Cornish at www.stavka.photos*)

Behind the lines logistics units often struggled to keep supplies rolling forwards at the pace they were required. As the Soviet General Staff study noted, 'In the conditions of the wooded and swampy terrain and the lack of roads … covered 22kms.' Such a move would require a massive effort to provide sufficient supplies to maintain the advance's momentum. (*Courtesy of the Central Museum of the Armed Forces, Moscow via Stavka*)

Their helmets covered by mosquito nets, this German gun team receives ammunition resupply. Their position looks solid enough to provide sufficient cover from small arms fire but little else. *(Nik Cornish at www.stavka.photos)*

The heavy black smoke of an oil fire in Polotsk railway station. Such destruction led to the Red Army's increasing reliance on motor vehicles, of which huge numbers were Lend-Lease Studebaker US6 six-wheel-drive trucks. (*Nik Cornish at www.stavka.photos*)

An unidentified German officer pictured just before he undergoes interrogation. The men of his unit are to the right. They were captured on the road north-west of Polotsk by men of Third Baltic Front on 3 July. (*Courtesy of the Central Museum of the Armed Forces, Moscow via Stavka*)

There were very few occasions during Operation Bagration where Soviet tankers were unable to recover and repair damaged tanks. This was due to the fact that they were advancing and therefore the repair and maintenance teams, such as the one pictured here, were able to get to work promptly. Note the external, auxiliary fuel tank being topped up. The major problem was the replacement of experienced crews. (*From the fonds of the RGAKFD in Krasnogorsk via Stavka*)

Chapter Seven

Model Takes Command

Generalfeldmarschall Walter Model was to a certain extent to blame for the poor condition of AGC when Bagration began, having, with Hitler and OKH's approval, stripped it of virtually all of its armoured formations. Now he was in the position of having to deal with the situation that had ensued. In this he was in a more advantageous position than Busch due to the fact that, as well as commanding AGC, Model also retained command of AGNU. This dual role enabled Model to facilitate the movement of units from AGNU to support AGC. Model's former Chief of Staff, *Oberstgeneral* Josef Harpe, became AGNU's temporary commander (in German military parlance 'Entrusted with command').

Model was not one to blindly follow the Führer's orders to the letter whatever the situation; he would bend the orders where necessary. In addition, unlike Busch, Model had faith in himself and his abilities and was prepared to make decisions without always consulting higher authority until the deed was done. Earlier in the war, when discussing Model with an adjutant, Hitler said, 'I trust the man to do it. But I don't want to serve under him myself.'

The replacement of Busch with Model confirmed OKH's acceptance of the seriousness of the Soviet offensive facing AGC and reinforcements were already on their way from AGNU. Of two Heavy Panzer Battalions, 505th and 507th, the latter entrained for Baranovichi, south-west of Minsk, on 23–24 June, where it was deployed to cover the arrival of 4th Panzer Division that Model hoped to transfer from AGNU. The 505th was sent to Borisov, some 70km east of Minsk, a vitally important crossing point on the Berezina River for the Moscow–Minsk highway and rail line. Further to the east along the highway lay Krupki on the Bobr River. It was in Krupki where the 505th took position on the Bobr's west bank along the railway line.

The importance of these crossing points to the forces of Third Panzer and Fourth Armies was crucial and the deployment of the forty or so Tiger Is with the 505th underscored this. Almost immediately, during the night of 27–28 June, around Krupki one of the companies of the 505th was in action. Later, in the morning of 28 June, elements of Fifth Guards Tank Army joined the fray.

Another formation deployed to cover the Moscow–Minsk highway was *Kampfgruppe Gottberg*, made up of Belarusian, Latvian, Lithuanian, Ukrainian and Cossack collaborationist security units as well as German police formations. Having been employed until mid-June on anti-partisan operations, *Gottberg*'s units were part of Third Panzer Army's reserve. *ObergruppenFührer* von Gottberg, a favourite of Himmler, had been appointed commander of the anti-partisan operations in Belarus and had waged a ruthless war against the partisans and anyone he regarded as their supporters for many months. By 27 June Gottberg's force had fallen back towards the Berezina bridges at Borisov. However, Gottberg refused to integrate his forces into *Kampfgruppe Saucken* (*Generalmajor* Dietrich von Saucken) as it was a Wehrmacht not an SS formation. During the brief time his units were at Borisov, Gottberg's men continued to execute suspected partisans, who appear to have been Belarusians hoping to depart with the Germans.

During the evening of 28 June, Busch had informed Third Panzer Army's commander, *Generaloberst* Rheinhardt, and General Tippelskirch, commanding Fourth Army, that Model now commanded AGC. Having reached AGC's HQ in Minsk (he would later remove it to Brest Litovsk) on 29 June, Model contacted Rheinhardt to find out what he needed to maintain a continuous front with AGN. Rheinhardt believed that *Kampfgruppe Saucken*, based on elements of XXXIX Panzer Corps, which at this point essentially consisted of 5th Panzer Division together with the Heavy Panzer Battalion 505, could help cover the northern flank of Third Panzer Army and support the other forces in the area along with the AGN-AGC connection as well as the Borisov crossing points.

Having been thoroughly briefed, Model set about tackling the overall situation. He clarified that Fourth Army's mission was to, 'get its divisions back behind the Berezina River in as battle worthy a condition as possible while the reinforcement of the echelons on both flanks continues. Contact with Ninth Army's eastern flank is to be established and maintained (around the town of Cherven, some 65km south-east of Minsk). This defence line is to be pulled back to the road behind the Berezina River on both sides of Borisov. This would free 5th Panzer Division in case of emergency to be employed west of the Berezina River … There is no available garrison for Borisov. Borisov is to be incorporated into the forming of a defensive front as a strongpoint.' By this reasoning Borisov, designated as a *Feste Platz*, would not be treated as such, thus avoiding the possibility of losing yet more troops in a futile gesture.

Model also ordered Ninth Army, in the process of merging with Second Army, to use the 12th Panzer Division, just arrived from AGNU, to block the Soviet advance south-east of Minsk while 20th Panzer Division continued to try and clear a route for the escapees from Bobruisk.

Discussions between OKH and AGC led to the redeployment of 4th Panzer and 28th Jager Divisions from AGNU to the Baranovichi–Slutsk area south of Minsk. Transferred from AGN, the 132nd and 170th Infantry Divisions would reinforce the Minsk and Molodechno areas, 75km north-west of Minsk, respectively. Finally, 7th Panzer Division (from AGNU) would move to Baranovichi, 145km to the south-west of Minsk and 113km west of Slutsk. Clearly, Model was laying down the line he hoped to defend west of Minsk, without directly stating it to OKH and risking the Führer's wrath. The position at Molodechno would cover the main road into Lithuania and that at Baranovichi the approaches to Poland as well as covering the flanks of AGNU and AGN, the latter now threatened with being isolated altogether should Third Baltic Front be ordered to dash towards the Baltic Sea. Interestingly, Model's chosen line of defence ran through an area that had seen heavy fighting and fortification during the First World War and through which ran an intermediary defence line that the Soviet General Staff study described as being in, 'a dilapidated condition and had only been partially restored'. In other words, it posed only a little problem. Nevertheless, it was better than nothing for the men of AGC.

As the various corps of Fourth Army moved towards the Berezina River bridges at the town of Beresino, Tippelskirch met with *Generalleutnant* Vincenz Muller, commander of the still relatively intact XII AC, at Beresino on 1 July. The purpose of the meeting was to place Muller in command of the unified VI, XII and XXXIX Panzer Corps that became *Kampfgruppe Muller*. Tippelskirch's final advice to Muller was to ease the retreat by abandoning materiel and vehicles to keep the road to Beresino as physically empty as possible. XXXIX Panzer Corps' HQ staff was transferred to *Kampfgruppe Saucken* to provide it with a staff capable of managing a formation of that size effectively. Muller was to rely on the staff of his own corps. Fourth Army's situation was summed up by its Chief of Staff thus, 'Lack of information on the flanking armies' situation makes it impossible for the Fourth Army to judge whether there is a risk of the enemy developing a third encircling ring with pincers meeting about in the region of Minsk. The large gap on Third Panzer Army's right leads one to suppose that there is no way of stopping an advance on Minsk … especially from the north. The extraordinary degree of enemy air superiority … combined with his superiority in tanks and the constant threat to our flanks has resulted not only in the dismemberment of a united front … a considerable deterioration of combat worth but also a sharp decline in morale … The difficult terrain east of the Berezina River … has given rise to irreplaceably high losses of vehicles and precious materials. Losses among commanders are terrible. XXXIX Panzer Corps has lost three [it was two, Martinek and Schunemann but VI AC had also lost its commander on 28 June] commanding generals within twenty-four hours. Only a few formations are still firmly under their commanders' control.'

Kampfgruppe Muller's rearguard units were fighting as best they could some 30km east of the Berezina River as Fourth Army disintegrated around and ahead of them. As Fourth Army relocated its HQ several times following very difficult journeys during which communications were severely disrupted, Muller was to remain effectively its commander until 8 July.

Less than a week earlier, Tippelskirch's staff had wondered where a force of 120 Soviet tanks had been headed and suddenly the answer became horrifically obvious. This armour was part of Third Belarusian Front's Cavalry-Mechanised Group and, by 29 June, its forward elements had crossed the Berezina River north of Borisov, with infantry support provided by Fifth Army following closely behind. Rotmistrov's Fifth Guards Tank Army was also battering its way towards Borisov despite the strong resistance from *Kampfgruppe Saucken*'s Panthers and Tigers. With the threat of the Cavalry-Mechanised Group advancing along the Berezina's western bank into its rear and Rotmistrov's armour coming almost directly towards them, Saucken's forces were in a difficult position. Furthermore, by 1 July, troops of Eleventh Guards Army were crossing the Berezina south of Borisov having advanced more slowly due to its involvement in mopping-up operations to the rear of the breakthrough forces. Consequently, to avoid encirclement, *Kampfgruppe Saucken* was ordered to withdraw to the west covering Molodechno and Minsk along with the 110th Infantry Division. The latter had crossed the Berezina with elements of the 'Wandering Pocket' that included *Feldherrnhalle*, 78th Assault, 57th and 337th Infantry Divisions, Heavy Panzer Battalion 501's few remaining Tigers and staff groups from XXVII and XXXIX Panzer Corps a dozen kilometres north of Beresino. There the *Kampfgruppe Saucken* would join up with 170th Infantry Division on its way by rail from AGN. The units that had crossed with the 110th were lucky to have avoided the growing traffic jam at Beresino and along its approach roads.

The bridge in Borisov was covered by a rearguard with orders to blow the main bridge, which they did in spite of the best efforts of a Soviet 'Forlorn Hope' comprising four T-34s from III Guards Tank Brigade that attempted to prevent its destruction. Despite that, the Fifth Guards Tank Army began to cross, by pontoons, to liberate Borisov on 1 July. With the fall of Borisov, a major escape route for Third Panzer and Fourth Armies was lost. Furthermore, as the streets of the town rang with the noise of street fighting, the last significant obstacle before Minsk, the Berezina River, was lost to Model.

As it withdrew from the south of Borisov, *Kampfgruppe Gottberg* was subordinated to Fourth Army's VI AC to hold the road from Borisov to Minsk. However, Gottberg once again refused to subordinate his SS units to the Army and twenty-four hours later he announced that his men had been broken by the Soviets. Having instructed all police formations to gather to him, he refused yet another order, this time to defend Vilnius, the capital of Lithuania, and fell back to positions at Lida, 200km or so west of Minsk. Gottberg's men accomplished this retreat by 6 July. Remarkably, by the middle of August Gottberg had been promoted, received a Knight's Cross and command of XII SS AC.

Having liberated Borisov, Third Belarusian Front's Cavalry-Mechanised Group was now ordered to direct its armour towards Vileyka and its cavalry towards Molodechno, the capture of which would cut communications between Minsk and Vilnius. The intention was to take both areas by 2 July. Faced with little in the way of opposition bar the odds and ends of local collaborationist security battalions, progress was swift and Vileyka fell on 2 July. The cavalry faced more powerful resistance but, with the support of Eleventh Guards Army, took its objective on 5 July. However, the failure by the cavalry to achieve its goal on time led to the Cavalry-Mechanised Group being taken back under the direct control of the Front commander and, in the words of the Red Army Staff Study, it, 'ceased to exist as a major mobile field force for operational purposes'. However, at this stage of the war neither of the Cavalry-Mechanised Group's corps commanders was punished.

As Third Belarusian Front was now crossing the Berezina on a broad front, Chernyakhovsky issued the following orders to Fifth Guards Tank Army. 'Co-operating with Thirty First Army [to the north and north-east of Minsk] and II Guards Tatinsky Tank Corps, it is to capture Minsk from the east and south-east.' The deadline for this outcome was midnight on 3 July.

While all the above had been going on, First Belarusian Front had hardly been idle. Its Cavalry-Mechanised Group was pushing towards Slutsk, which was taken on 30 June and, by dawn on 2 July, it had cut Minsk off from Brest-Litovsk and Baranovichi. Equally important was the link up of Third Army's XXXV Rifle Corps with units of Second Belarusian Front's Forty-Ninth Army near Cherven (Tscherwen on German maps) on the Minsk–Mogilev high road west of Beresino, some 65km east of Minsk. This, at first tenuous, connection, was the beginning of the envelopment of much of Fourth and Ninth Armies' troops in two huge pockets east and west of the Beresino crossing points. Outside of Minsk, on its southern approaches, a blocking position was held by the remains of 14th Infantry Division, elements of 31st Infantry and 12th Infantry Divisions along with some odds and ends of other units with a few heavy weapons that had coalesced into *Kampfgruppe Florke*, named for the commander of the 14th Infantry Division. *Kampfgruppe Florke* pulled back towards Minsk but, finding the city being evacuated, moved out and finally linked up with 12th Panzer Division. Florke's troops, along with *Kampfgruppe Saucken* to the north of Minsk, were able to hold the Soviet forces for long enough to allow for the escape of three hospital trains carrying some 8,000 wounded and over forty evacuation trains bearing many thousands of rear-echelon personnel to the west on 1 and 2 July. Model, having concluded defending Minsk was a lost cause, had sanctioned the evacuation of the wounded and other troops from the city. Symptomatic of this conclusion was the decision to send Heavy Tank Battalion 507 from AGNU to Molodechno to bolster the growing defences west of Minsk, where it arrived on 2 July.

Despite its status as a *Feste Platz*, the defences of Minsk were virtually non-existent. The garrison consisted of some 1,800 disorganised troops and up to 15,000 stragglers, largely unarmed and disoriented, who had reached the city. Demolition of key installations began on 1 July and, with Hitler's acquiescence, the evacuation became official the following day. The Commandant of the city was Luftwaffe *Generalleutnant* Sperling, who had held the post since 1942. He too was evacuated.

Elsewhere, the tank-less Third Panzer Army, now effectively reduced to LIII AC having transferred IX AC to AGN and VI AC to Fourth Army, remained under the command of Rheinhardt but was, as a unified body, almost non-existent and what remained was more a part of AGN than AGC.

While Ninth Army's remnants, reduced to a *Kampfgruppe* led by Panzer General Nikolaus von Vormann and subordinate to Weiß's Second Army, were falling back along the northern bank of the Pripet River, some of its units were swept away by Fourth Army towards Minsk.

As the largest, relatively, cohesive body, Fourth Army was now facing destruction as the encirclement tightened around what was in effect a selection of artillery and aircraft targets and, as more and more Soviet units arrived from the rear, infantry formations were told to increase the solidity of the encirclement. Not only Minsk was about to fall but Fourth Army was facing its own Cannae.

GFM Walter Model (holding map), pictured here in May 1944, took command of AGC on 28 June 1944. By this time he had gained a reputation with Hitler and the OKH as a stabiliser of endangered fronts and a master of defence, earning the nickname of 'Hitler's Fireman'. He was also capable of 'overlooking' Hitler's more extreme demands for holding ground. However, he was not popular with many of his subordinates. (*Nik Cornish at www.stavka.photos*)

On the right is GFM Ernst Busch when commander of Sixteenth Army under AGN's leader GFM von Leeb (arm on hip) in 1941. Transferred to AGC in late 1943, Busch was not a confident Army commander. When Model replaced him, Busch, personally aggrieved by his dismissal, did not brief him personally. Busch was not active again until April 1945. (*Nik Cornish at www.stavka.photos*)

On 29 June elements of 5th Panzer Division and roughly forty Tigers of Heavy Tank Battalion 505 clashed with Rotmistrov's Fifth Guards Tank Army east of Borisov. The Soviets were taken by surprise and suffered up to 50 per cent losses. This holding action blunted the speed of the Soviet advance and gained time for Fourth Army's withdrawal to proceed. Some of the last units to arrive were engaged by Soviet forces as they were offloading from their trains. (*Nik Cornish at www.stavka.photos*)

T-34/76s of Fifth Guards Tank Army. This is the 1943 version with the box-type fuel tanks to the rear. The repulse at Borisov provided Stavka with another reason to criticise Rotmistrov. However, as his armour continued to advance, many of the damaged tanks were recovered and repaired. (*From the fonds of the RGAKFD in Krasnogorsk via Stavka*)

As well as being used for casualty evacuation, the U-2/Po-2 was also deployed to drop propaganda leaflets on German columns and pockets when flying daylight recconnaissance missions. These leaflets were produced by the National Committee for a Free Germany, a group of German communist exiles that was later joined by a number of German officers. The main activity was persuasion work at the front with the aim of persuading members of the Wehrmacht to defect or to be taken prisoner voluntarily. (*Courtesy of the Central Museum of the Armed Forces, Moscow via Stavka*)

The results of Soviet propaganda were often fruitful. German stragglers would hide until rear-echelon troops appeared and surrender to them rather than combat units of *Frontoviki* (Front Line men), who were less likely to be merciful. (*Courtesy of the Central Museum of the Armed Forces, Moscow via Stavka*)

The road that the bulk of Fourth Army's divisions used to reach the Beresino bridgehead rapidly became jammed with vehicles of all types up to three abreast. At its height the jam was reported to be 60km in length. This image taken by the Red Army some days after the fall of Minsk gives an idea of what the chaos must have been like before a considerable amount of clearance work had been carried out by German POWs, civilians hunting for loot and Red Army engineers who salvaged anything of value. Many perfectly good vehicles were abandoned simply for lack of fuel. *(Courtesy of the Central Museum of the Armed Forces, Moscow via Stavka)*

Troopers of a unit of First Belarusian Front's Cavalry-Mechanised Group canter through relatively unscathed countryside in early July. The value of these units, which could bypass roads and tracks clogged with wrecked vehicles, was immense. To almost all German troops Soviet cavalry were referred to as *Kossaken* and the cry of '*Die Kossaken kommen*' was often enough to create panic. *(From the fonds of the RGAKFD in Krasnogorsk via Stavka)*

Late on 30 June the Beresino crossings were under direct fire from Soviet artillery. These are M1939 76mm USB divisional guns. With a maximum range of over 13km and a crew of five, it was a useful weapon in such circumstances. (*From the fonds of the RGAKFD in Krasnogorsk via Stavka*)

To provide infantrymen, clerks, cooks and any other able-bodied men from the rear echelons were ordered forwards to man the front line. Manning an MG 34, these two men have their hand grenades close by. (*Nik Cornish at www.stavka.photos*)

German forces on the Eastern Front came to rely more and more over the years on local vehicles such as the ubiquitous panje (panje refers to the horse type), wagon as seen here. Pulled by teams of locally bred horses that could survive on the barest of fodder, they were infinitely more reliable than motor vehicles in the terrain many of AGC's units had to negotiate during the weeks of Operation Bagration. (*Nik Cornish at www.stavka.photos*)

Often overlooked is the role played by cavalry formations during the summer of 1944. Although fielding far fewer cavalry than their opponents, AGC's Second Army's cavalry was deployed to good effect during the collapse of AGC. Such mobile, off-road forces proved highly effective at covering the retreat of other formations that lacked their mobility. (*Nik Cornish at www.stavka.photos*)

A Lend-Lease Valentine of III Guards Mechanised Corps heads for the Berezina River on 29 June. This unit was supported by III Guards Cavalry Corps but that force had advanced more slowly as it faced stubborn resistance. Armoured elements of the Cavalry-Mechanised Group now began to move south, when fuel supplies permitted, to threaten *Kampfgruppe Saucken*'s northern defences around Borisov. (*Courtesy of the Central Museum of the Armed Forces, Moscow via Stavka*)

Luftflotte 6 stepped up its support of the ground troops, to the north and south of the Borisov bridgehead, at the end of June by attacking the Red Army bridgeheads. However, the losses incurred, such as this Fw 190, reduced their capabilities even further. (*From the fonds of the RGAKFD in Krasnogorsk via Stavka*)

The arrival of 5th Panzer Division at Borisov provided a huge boost for AGC consisting of seventy Panzer VI Panthers and fifty-five Panzer IVs. Unfortunately the armour was the last element to arrive other than the Tiger Is of Heavy Panzer Battalion 505. When Borisov was lost, 5th Panzer Division fell back along the highway to screen Minsk. By 8 July all the Tigers had been lost and the division reduced to just over 10 per cent of its armour during costly engagements with Fifth Guards Tank Army. (*Nik Cornish at www.stavka.photos*)

Soviet engineers were supplied with various types of boats to facilitate the crossing of the innumerable Belarusian waterways. This is a type DDP, which was designed to be a part of a light pontoon bridge but could be used as shown here. (*Nik Cornish at www.stavka.photos*)

The Pioneers of 110th Infantry Division were tasked with building two bridges over the Berezina River. It was over these bridges that the Wandering Pocket that included elements of *Feldherrnhalle*, 78th Sturm, 110th, 157th and 337th Infantry Divisions as well as other units crossed to the river's western bank by 2 July. As they moved west, they did receive some airdrops of fuel but only sufficient for staff and wounded transport. (*Nik Cornish at www.stavka.photos*)

On both banks of the Berezina River, Fourth Army's pockets were the targets Red Army artillerymen never imagined they would have. Despite being based on a design from 1909, this 152mm howitzer was in service until 1945. (*Nik Cornish at www.stavka.photos*)

Chapter Eight

The Fall of Minsk and the Aftermath

Fourth Army had pulled back towards the bridges at Beresino but now found itself isolated, cut off from ground supply since midday on 1 July and with its corps to HQ communications either broken, jammed or intermittent. Muller, its field commander, was rarely able to contact the Fourth Army's commander due to Tippelskirch's frequent HQ relocations and when the last report of 1 July was sent to AGC HQ it read, 'Fighting heroically on all sides in places against a closely pursuing enemy with superior forces, the army's last divisions are trying to fight their way back to the Berezina River despite shortages of ammunition, rations and fuel.' However, communications had been restored with VI AC but not to XXVII AC, which, it was believed, was somewhere about 50km to the north-east of Beresino. By this time the bridgehead had contracted to roughly 20 sq km as there was little artillery ammunition to keep the Soviets at bay.

Throughout the night of 1–2 July, men and essential machines crossed the river at Beresino and finally at 1845hrs on 2 July Muller reported to Fourth Army HQ that his divisions had crossed the river except for the rearguards, adding that his men had the, 'complete confidence' and the 'will to break through' towards the north-east of Minsk. Tippelskirch replied, 'The progress of the corps is followed with a fervent heart. We are doing everything to help that we can with our limited resources.' Unfortunately one of these resources was *Kampfgruppe Florke*, which was in the process of pulling back from the town precisely where Muller's forces had been hoping to link up and resupply. However, this was not now possible. At 0815hrs the next day Muller was notified by radio that the, 'Situation in Minsk is unclear … and *Kampfgruppe Florke* was endangered.' In fact, Minsk was on the point of falling and Florke's men had left.

For the ordinary German troops cut off behind enemy lines, Minsk's fate was generally unknown. For many, especially those east of the Berezina River, their own futures were of far greater importance. The feelings of those to the west of the Berezina were similar. Many felt let down that there was no defensive line behind the river, which would have provided some respite and even an opportunity to hold the Soviet flood. In the pockets that they now found themselves in, they took cover and put their faith in their officers.

The liberation of Minsk is described by Zhukov in his memoirs as follows: 'At dawn on July 3, the II Guards Tank Corps of A.S. Burdeyny burst into Minsk from the north-east; from the north, the advanced units of the Fifth Guards Tank Army of Marshal of the Armoured Forces P.A. Rotmistrov approached the city. In the middle of the day the city was entered by the I Guards Tank Corps of the First Belarusian Front under the command of General M.F. Panov. Following the tank corps of M.F. Panov, the Third Army of General A.V. Gorbatov approached the outskirts of Minsk … Towards the end, on July 3, the main group of formations of the Fourth Army of German troops found themselves cut off from the escape routes and trapped east of Minsk … By the end of July 3, Minsk was completely cleared of the enemy.'

On 4 July Third Belarusian Front's combat report recorded somewhat laconically, 'The forces of the Third Belarusian Front, as a result of a rapid offensive and deep outflanking manoeuvre from the north-west, have occupied the enemy's very important strategic defensive centre along the western direction – the capital of Soviet Belarus, Minsk.'

Whereas Stavka announced it as follows, 'The troops of the Third Belarusian Front, with the assistance of the troops of the First Belarusian Front, as a result of a deep enveloping manoeuvre, stormed the capital of Soviet Belarus, the city of Minsk – the most important strategic hub of the German defence in the western direction.' In fact, the honours for the liberation of Minsk were divided between First, Second and Third Belarusian Fronts.

During the day Soviet troops rounded up what remained of Mink's garrison and those left behind and, by late evening, Soviet tanks were already 10–15km west of the city.

On the morning of 3 July Muller assembled his senior officers to consider the direction and nature of a breakout from the encirclement. Apparently there was no discussion of surrender. When the meeting ended, having drawn up a plan for the breakout attempt, Muller radioed Fourth Army HQ noting the problems facing his units. He informed it that, 'Despite stringent measures, heavy congestion occurs and as a result signs of disaffection among the vast numbers of stragglers are evident. There exist no more possibilities to concentrate combat troops and artillery with ammunition rapidly enough for a planned attack because of movement problems. Therefore I have decided and ordered the breakout of the threatened encirclement with as many men of sound morale as possible with basic weapons heading south of Minsk to the west.' Apparently, Muller was so confident of extricating his command successfully that he is quoted as saying, 'It would be hilarious if we weren't chasing these pigs through the sun, moon and stars.'

Model's orders for Fourth Army related to Muller's divisions in as much as he urged, 'By conducting a sufficient anti-tank defence to make possible a rallying point for the elements of Fourth Army still east of the Berezina.' Muller's troops were, so it seems from that order, to have been written off. Muller was officially informed of the loss of Minsk at 1710hrs on 3 July.

Second Belarusian Front's Fiftieth Army supported by First Belarusian Front's Third Army were tasked with, as Rokossovsky put it, 'The mopping up of the Nazi troops in the Minsk pocket.'

Unfortunately for the men of *Kampfgruppe Muller*, the breakout attempt ended in failure; they simply did not have the resources to make any impression on the Soviet lines. The 25th Panzer Grenadier Division had somehow kept thirty StuG IIIs and twenty self-

of our trap and work their way westward toward the forests. Our duty ... is to prevent the Germans from reaching the forests ...'

Officially, the 'clean up', as Soviet sources described it, ended on 12 July, although unofficially it continued for some weeks. German sources estimate some 9,000 *Ruckkampfer* made it back to German lines by the late summer, although establishing accurate German losses is problematic to say the least. However, 300,000–350,000 seems to a reasonable figure. Suffice it to say that AGC had lost a catastrophic number of men killed, wounded, missing and captured. Russian researchers accept that German losses were overestimated during the Soviet period but, in 2007, Russian sources put the Soviet losses for Bagration at 178,507 dead, missing and captured, as well as 587,308 wounded and sick.

Among the German POWs were nineteen officers of general rank. Of these, seventeen were to join the Soviet-sponsored National Committee for Free Germany, an anti-Nazi German Communist movement: this was the largest defection of German officers to date.

The liberation of Minsk led Stavka to update its plans for the next phase of Operation Bagration.

First Baltic Front was to advance towards Latvia and Lithuania with the general idea of isolating AGN by reaching the Baltic Sea. The offensive began on 5 July as reinforcements were expected to maintain the momentum of the advance.

To the right of First Baltic Front, Third Belarusian Front was ordered to push towards Vilnius and establish bridgeheads on the western bank of the Neman River. The Fifth Guards Tank Army was to support the move on Vilnius by edging northwards. The Cavalry-Mechanised Group would move towards the Neman and, again, operations commenced on 5 July.

Second Belarusian Front could only contribute its Third Army due to mopping-up work. Nevertheless, on 5 July, it too was ordered to move westwards.

First Belarusian Front's right-flank troops were to advance on Baranovichi and press AGC's Second Army westwards. However, it was now deemed appropriate to involve the Front's left-flank forces against AGNU in the direction of Kovel and those forces joined Operation Bagration during the first week of July.

Now OKH had an even greater set of challenges to face as the whole of its Eastern Front was to be set ablaze, the last thing the Wehrmacht needed was internal dissension.

As AGC, AGN and AGNU were fighting for their lives to the east, at Hitler's HQ in the East Prussian forests to their rear an attempt was made on the Führer's life on 20 July. The events surrounding the 'Bomb Plot' (as this attempt would become known) and its consequences have no place here but there is one episode that exemplifies the confusion to the rear of AGC at that time, the ride of the 31st Cavalry Regiment of the 3rd Cavalry Brigade. The regiment's commander, *Oberstleutnant* Philip Boeselager, along with his brother Georg (his brigade commander) and other officers of these units, had been members of the conspiracy to assassinate Hitler for almost two years. Their involvement in the Bomb Plot was remarkable. Philip would lead six squadrons, 1,200 troopers, from where they would be trucked from Brest-Litovsk to Warsaw and then flown to Berlin to arrest Himmler and Goebbels and take over the Reich Security Ministry! On 18 July they were ordered to move out, riding 200km in thirty-six hours. They were then notified that the attempt had failed and that they should return to their former positions, which they did, unnoticed. Luckily, the conspirators that were arrested did not disclose the brothers' involvement and they continued in their roles. Georg was killed in action five weeks later, however, Philip survived the war, dying in 2008. Officially, the unit was noted as 'missing' during this time and, such was the chaotic situation, the reappearance of 1,200 combat veterans was greeted with pleasure, not suspicion.

The liberation of Minsk and the catastrophic collapse of AGC marked the end of Hitler's eastern ambitions as now Soviet troops were set fair to drive into the Balkans, the Baltic States and enter the sacred ground of the Reich itself. The next phase of Operation Bagration would set the stage for the Soviet invasion of Greater Germany and would soon see the Red Army at the gates of Warsaw.

Not all Belarusians were pro-Soviet, however. During the summer of 1943 the Union of Belarussian Youth (UBY), modelled on the Hitler Youth, was officially recognised by the occupation authorities. It had been formed roughly a year earlier to spread support for anti-Soviet activities and pro-German propaganda. The UBY members wore a brassard in the national colours of red and white. More than 10,000 members were recorded in mid-1944, many of whom retreated with the Germans and joined the Wehrmacht, often as anti-aircraft gunners. Others remained behind and joined the rapidly increasing number of partisans hoping to avoid discovery. (*From the fonds of the RGAKFD in Krasnogorsk via Stavka*)

A group of mounted partisans entering a recently liberated town are welcomed by the inhabitants. However, there was always a noticeable tension between those who had joined the partisans in the early days and those who had remained on the fence. Few, if any males, can be seen in the civilian crowd. (*Courtesy of the Central Museum of the Armed Forces, Moscow via Stavka*)

When a town or village was taken by the Red Army, a screen of infantry was usually left to guard any roads or paths that passed through or nearby to intercept any German troops who had fallen behind their unit. Here one such lightly armed group, covered by a machine gun, goes in pursuit of German stragglers. (*From the fonds of the RGAKFD in Krasnogorsk via Stavka*)

Soviet artillery moves along the Moscow–Minsk high road. The gun is a Model 1931/37 122mm. This is being towed by a Stalinets S-65 tractor. Stalin is quoted as saying that artillery was 'the god of war'. (*Nik Cornish at www.stavka.photos*)

Before Operation Bagration the NKVD had launched Operation Sejm with the simple objective of undermining the Polish resistance movement, the Home Army (the AK), before it could influence events in former Polish areas of Belarus. When Red Army units came into contact with the AK they were to 'encourage' AK members into joining the Polish People's Army, a part of the Red Army. This image shows new Polish recruits (right) with their new comrades. (*Courtesy of the Central Museum of the Armed Forces, Moscow via Stavka*)

Heavy Tank Battalion 505 lost nine Tigers at Krupki and Borisov. The somewhat dispersed Heavy Tank Battalion 501 managed to get about six across the Berezina River by ferry on 1 or 2 July but received another five from the Minsk repair facility. However, three days later the latter battalion's last Tigers were destroyed by their crews when they ran out of fuel. (*Nik Cornish at www.stavka.photos*)

Leutnantgeneral Vincenz Muller with General I.V. Boldin, commander of Fiftieth Army. According to his account, Muller, 'accompanied by one officer and a bugler, I rode out on horseback from our location and headed at random towards the Russians … we came across the guards of the headquarters of a large artillery formation; I was immediately escorted to one of the senior Soviet officers … I told him about the situation in the cauldron and stated that I wanted to give an order to stop resistance, but I no longer had the means to convey this order to my subordinates.' (*Courtesy of the Central Museum of the Armed Forces, Moscow via Stavka*)

Men of *Kampfgruppe Muller* surrender to a partisan unit. (*Courtesy of the Central Museum of the Armed Forces, Moscow via Stavka*)

On Sunday, 16 July thirty partisan brigades paraded on the old racecourse in Minsk, headed by Malysh, a goat carrying German medals. Watched by some 50,000 spectators, roughly 30,000 partisans, led by their standard bearers, marched, as one participant put it, 'proudly with awards on their chests! They were winners!' The spectators included many local party officials as well as the commander of the Third Belarusian Front, General of the Army I. D. Chernyakhovsky. The majority of the partisans were then transferred to the Red Army. (*Courtesy of the Central Museum of the Armed Forces, Moscow via Stavka*)

The Secretary of the Vitebsk Communist Party region (right) interviews civilians on his return to the city. (*Courtesy of the Central Museum of the Armed Forces, Moscow via Stavka*)

On 5 July air supply for Fourth Army ended. The last supply packages were dropped near Smilawitschy, 27km south-east of Minsk on the Orsha–Minsk high road. These were happily distributed among the men of I Guards Motorised Brigade, part of Rokossovsky's I Guards Tank Corps, which had arrived there on 3 July. The view is from the side window of a Ju 52 transport plane. (*Nik Cornish at www.stavka.photos*)

Men of the *Feldjägerkorps*, an infinitely more powerful, combat experienced version of the *Feldgendarmerie*, that was formed in November 1943. Their major roles were the maintenance of discipline, the prevention of panicked retreats and the rounding up and organisation of stragglers – a hard task during the summer of 1944. (*Nik Cornish at www.stavka.photos*)

A wrecked T-34/76 Model 1943 tank with a cupola on the turret that dates it to late 1943. The POW and guard are accompanied by a local collaborator. Any POWs were regarded as invaluable sources of intelligence. (*Nik Cornish at www.stavka.photos*)

Inside the Wandering Pockets, for the *Kampfgruppen* and the innumerable bands of isolated German troops, every day was one of hope coupled with desperation. (*Nik Cornish at www.stavka.photos*)

Marshal Vasilevsky stated: 'On 5 July I visited Minsk. The impression I was left with was extremely difficult. The city was heavily destroyed by the Nazis. Of the large buildings, the enemy did not manage to blow up only the house of the Belarusian government, the new building of the Central Committee of the Communist Party of Belarus, the radio plant and the House of the Red Army. The power plant, railway station, most industrial enterprises and institutions were blown up.' Some of the of the city's children in the remains of their home. (*From the fonds of the RGAKFD in Krasnogorsk via Stavka*)

For one unit of the Red Army, the 129th Rifle Division, its participation in Operation Bagration garnered it another award to add to its honorific title 'Orlovskaya' for its role in the liberation of Orel less than twelve months earlier. For successful battles to liberate Belarus, including completing the encirclement of 'the enemy's Bobruisk grouping', the division was awarded the Order of the Red Banner on 19 August 1944. Here two of the division's men read about the award in the unit news. (*Courtesy of the Central Museum of the Armed Forces, Moscow via Stavka*)

Known popularly as the 'Parade of the Vanquished' or 'Operation Big Waltz' (one of Stalin's favourite films) by its NKVD organisers, the parade of 57,600 German officers and men through Moscow on 17 July 1944 demonstrated the Red Army's success to the ordinary people of the capital. It was also designed to embarrass Hitler by parodying his planned victory parade through Moscow. Every POW was examined and only those fit enough to march were paraded. The event was witnessed by more than 120,000 Muscovites. (*Courtesy of the Central Museum of the Armed Forces, Moscow via Stavka*)

Nineteen generals and six colonels led the parade. To the right is *Generalmajor* von Erdmannsdorff (the commander of Mogilev, who was executed for war crimes in early 1946). Centre, *Generalmajor* Gihr, commander 707th Infantry Division, while to the far right is *Generalmajor* Engel (commander 45th Infantry Division). Senior officers were permitted to wear their decorations and dress uniforms, whereas the others wore what they were captured in. The parade also demonstrated to those allies who had been sceptical of the Soviets, apparently outlandish, claims for Operation Bagration that they had achieved what they had claimed. (*From the fonds of the RGAKFD in Krasnogorsk via Stavka*)